T0305312

Mergers &
Acquisitions
Integration Handbook

Founded in 1807, John Wiley & Sons is the oldest independent publishing company in the United States. With offices in North America, Europe, Australia and Asia, Wiley is globally committed to developing and marketing print and electronic products and services for our customers' professional and personal knowledge and understanding.

The Wiley Finance series contains books written specifically for finance and investment professionals as well as sophisticated individual investors and their financial advisors. Book topics range from portfolio management to e-commerce, risk management, financial engineering, valuation and financial instrument analysis, as well as much more.

For a list of available titles, visit our Web site at www.WileyFinance.com.

Mergers & Acquisitions Integration Handbook

Helping Companies Realize the Full Value of Acquisitions

SCOTT C. WHITAKER

WILEY

John Wiley & Sons, Inc.

Published by John Wiley & Sons, Inc., Hoboken, New Jersey.
Published simultaneously in Canada.

For general information on our other products and services or for technical support, please contact our Customer Care Department within the United States at (800) 762-2974, outside the United States at (317) 572-3993 or fax (317) 572-4002.

Wiley also publishes its books in a variety of electronic formats. Some content that appears in print may not be available in electronic books. For more information about Wiley products, visit our web site at www.wiley.com.

Library of Congress Cataloging-in-Publication Data:

Whitaker, Scott C.
  Mergers & acquisitions integration handbook : helping companies realize the full value of acquisitions / Scott C. Whitaker.
      p. cm. – (Wiley finance series)
    title: Mergers and acquisitions integration handbook
    Includes index.
    ISBN 978-1-118-00437-1 (hardback); ISBN 978-1-118-22178-5 (ebk.);
    ISBN 978-1-118-23342-9 (ebk.); ISBN 978-1-118-26032-6
  1. Consolidation and merger of corporations. I. Title. II. Title: Mergers and acquisitions integration handbook.
  HD2746.5.W49 2012
  658.1'62–dc23

                        2012008099

Printed in the United States of America.

10 9 8 7 6 5 4 3 2 1

To my family, for supporting my efforts and always being there for me

Contents

Acknowledgments

I have had the great opportunity to work with some truly remarkable and talented people during my nearly 25 years as a professional. My career as an independent consultant has exposed me to some of the smartest business professionals all over the world, and I am forever grateful to all of you whom I have had the distinct pleasure of working with over the years.

I would also like to thank Matt Podowitz for contributing Chapter 14 on IT integration. Matt is an extremely gifted and talented professional, and readers will surely gain valuable insights from his breakdown of IT-related integration challenges and the role IT should play in post-merger integration.

CHAPTER 1

Introduction

If you are picking up this book, you have most likely been tasked with leading some integration-related endeavor for your company and are quickly trying to get up to speed and answer the call. Integration responsibilities are typically given to executives with a proven track record and a reputation for getting things done. If that's you, congratulations. But don't celebrate just yet. Now comes the hard part!

Integration takes many forms. It is defined as all the activities involved in bringing two corporate entities together after they have officially merged or after an acquisition by one company requires an integration of the acquired company into the first company. You might be doing a post-merger integration, a post-acquisition integration, or a partial integration; perhaps you don't even know the full extent of the project because it's still undefined. Regardless, it is imperative that integration work be effectively managed to preserve value and not disrupt business continuity, and that's what integration managers are typically supposed to accomplish.

This book provides a no-nonsense handbook-style approach to manage an effective integration and to help integration managers quickly get up to speed on various integration challenges and learn how to manage them. It is a desktop reference to inform your thinking and craft the optimal integration strategy for your company.

Since every company, industry, and deal is somewhat unique, there is no one-size-fits-all approach to integration. The best approach is typically a combination of various integration strategies, tools, and timing that best fit the task at hand.

WHO SHOULD USE THIS BOOK?

This handbook is intended for full-time employees who have been tasked with either of the following:

- Establishing an in-house integration management office or team to handle an upcoming integration or series of integrations.
- Managing an integration team (in-house and/or external consulting resources) in addition to their regular responsibilities.

For either of the above, this book is written to address integration deals valued at $250 million or less.

Although many of the principles and procedures outlined in this book can be applied to deals above $250 million, many companies that do large mergers or acquisitions typically hire large consulting firms to manage the bulk of the integration activities. These companies will employ many of the same integration strategies and tactics that are outlined in this book, but often the tools are proprietary and the engagements are long-term.

Many companies may choose to manage deals under $250 million in-house and task executives with the bulk of the day-to-day integration duties. If that executive is you, you've picked up the right book!

HOW THIS BOOK IS SET UP

This book is designed to address the most common integration activities and challenges. It is not intended to delve deeply into a particular industry or type of deal, but rather it addresses integration activities that are "industry and deal-size agnostic" and fairly ubiquitous to any merger or acquisition scenario.

The intent is to get the reader up to speed on the most common integration issues and to outline some basic practices to tackle integration projects in a rational and efficient manner that preserves and protects the value of your transaction.

This book also provides samples of tools and templates to illustrate how to accomplish many tasks, as well as suggested approaches to help you familiarize yourself with the topic.

The tools and templates used in this book to illustrate various integration activities are for illustration only. The optimal tool is the one that best matches the needs of *your* integration. Every integration is different, so be sure to develop tools and templates that are tailored to address your integration goals and deliverables.

CHAPTER SUMMARIES

Chapters 2 through 4 are an introduction to some merger and acquisition basics and some general planning guidelines and considerations for integration work. These chapters are intended to help readers understand the overall role of integration work and how to plan for integration.

Chapter 2, "Mergers and Acquisitions 101 and Assessing Integration Complexity and Risk": This chapter offers a short primer on some merger and acquisition basics, including tips on justifying and acquiring integration resources, understanding integration challenges, and laying the groundwork for your integration project.

Chapter 3, "Making the Business Case for Integration": This is a brief overview of how mergers and acquisitions are justified from a business perspective and how to make the business case for integration support.

Chapter 4, "An Introduction to Integration Planning": This is a summary of how the bulk of integration activities should be organized by phase in terms of key activities, desired outcomes, and risks.

Chapters 5 through 10 detail each major phase of integration and all of the key activities involved or recommended.

Chapter 5, "The Pre-Planning Phase": This chapter covers how to access the integration challenge and determine what resources are going to be required to manage it.

Chapter 6, "The Importance of Due Diligence": This chapter includes the topics of understanding the key aspects of the acquired company's organization, governance, and key business processes, along with helpful lists to get you started on collecting the inputs to support the development of the initial integration plan.

Chapter 7, "Establishing an Integration Management Office": This chapter covers establishing an integration management office (IMO) for the purposes of managing all integration activities.

Chapter 8, "Executing Your Integration Plan": Provides a summary of key activities related to the execution phase of integration, and included are numerous tools and templates to assist with execution tactics.

Chapter 9, "Planning Your Integration's End State": This chapter deals with the fact that every integration has to have an end. Planning for the end state is just as important as planning the integration itself.

Chapters 10 through 14 delve deeper into the most critical integration topics: communication planning, cultural integration, talent assessment, synergy program management, and information technology (IT) integration.

> Chapter 10, "Effective Communication Planning": This chapter offers the basic steps and practices to ensure that communication planning is a robust part of your integration.
>
> Chapter 11, "Cultural Integration and Assessment": This chapter warns you not to underestimate the challenge of integrating cultures. Integration and progress can be seriously impeded by culture clashes. Be prepared!
>
> Chapter 12, "The Talent Assessment Process" This chapter contains tools and practices to help you manage the most important part of any integration: people.
>
> Chapter 13, "Synergy Program Management": This chapter provides an overview of setting up a robust platform to manage and realize synergies that are part of your integration deliverables.
>
> Chapter 14, "Information Technology Integration": This chapter gives an overview of the critical role of IT and its importance in planning and executing a successful integration.

Chapters 15 and 16 are overviews of some common lessons I have learned from my previous integration work, and they include a summary of how to create an integration playbook to help companies manage ongoing integration activity.

> Chapter 15, "Integration Feedback: Lessons Learned": This chapter covers how to collect feedback from all stakeholder groups to continually optimize your integration strategies and tactics. Also included are some common lessons learned from previous integrations.
>
> Chapter 16, "Creating an Integration Playbook": This chapter covers how to create a scalable integration playbook for your organization.

A WORD TO THE WISE

Don't underestimate the task at hand. As you prepare for your upcoming integration, please remember the following:

■ *Every integration is the same but different.* Use this book to craft sound strategies and processes for effective integration management, but be flexible in accommodating the unique (and sometimes ever-changing) needs of your integration. Many integration challenges are the same regardless of deal size or industry, but they all have nuances that need tender care and focus.

- *Integrations are disruptive.* Expect your integration to disrupt operations and hamper business continuity. Do not underestimate the preparation and work required to manage a successful integration—they can be ugly, time-consuming, and contentious. Prepare for the worst and expect the best.
- *Integration is real work and requires competent people.* Make sure to staff your integration office properly (I will show you how later), and don't be caught shorthanded. Ask for more than you need up front, and when things get slow, you can adjust. If you need some short-term external resources, get them. Don't get caught shorthanded.
- *Have a bias for urgency.* Integrations should be accomplished as quickly as possible. Although some processes may take longer (e.g., plant consolidations), the bulk of integration activities should be able to be accomplished within a 60- to 120-day time frame. The longer an integration takes, the more disruptive and expensive it can be.
- *Overcommunicate.* We will discuss this at length, but you should assume that you will have to communicate everything five times or more. Poor communication is the most commonly cited pain point of most integrations.

I hope the rest of this handbook provides an ample supply of strategies, wisdom, insights, tools, processes, policies, and anecdotes to manage all of the things outlined here, along with anything else you're likely to encounter on your integration journey.

Good luck!

Mergers and Acquisitions 101 and Assessing Integration Complexity and Risk

In this chapter, you will learn how to do the following:

1. Determine the integration scope and the projected level of support activity required.
2. Justify and secure integration resources.
3. Understand the integration challenge.
4. Lay the groundwork for your integration project.

MERGERS AND ACQUISITIONS 101

Mergers and acquisitions (M&A) is a big part of the corporate finance world. Every day, investment bankers arrange M&A transactions to bring separate companies together to form larger ones. Deal valuations can be in the millions or even billions of dollars. However, they all require some degree of post-deal support to make them work, and that is what this book is about.*

A *merger* is a combination of two companies to form a new company, while an *acquisition* is the purchase of one company by another in which no new company is formed.

---

*Please note that this book is not intended to be a resource for extensive details on the financial aspects of mergers and acquisitions, as this book deals only with the activities that occur after a deal is completed.

The common scenarios for companies undertaking a merger or an acquisition include the following:

- A company cannot achieve double-digit sales growth organically.
- A company wants to take capacity out of the market (i.e., create industry consolidation).
- A company wants to expand its portfolio of products and services (i.e., create business diversification).
- The merger or acquisition is an opportunistic purchase.
- The merger or acquisition offers an opportunity to scale operations or consolidate them to achieve cost efficiencies.
- The merger or acquisition offers the opportunity for a technology play, creating competitive difference and the ability to jump on a fast-growth platform.
- The merger or acquisition plays into executive ego (e.g., makes a company a big fish or offers the ability to get on the cover of *Forbes*).
- It's a buy-or-be-bought situation (i.e., a company needs to achieve critical mass or to improve its stock price).

DETERMINING POST-ACQUISITION INTEGRATION SCOPE

An acquisition involves one firm purchasing another; one company buys most, if not all, of a target company's ownership stakes in order to assume control of the target firm. Acquisitions are necessary when companies seek economies of scale, efficiency, and enhanced market visibility, and they are often made as part of a company's growth strategy in which it is more beneficial to take over an existing firm's operations and niche compared to expanding on its own. Acquisitions are paid for with cash, stock, or a combination of the two, and they differ in terms of the necessary level of integration support.

All mergers and acquisitions have a common goal: they are meant to create synergy that makes the value of the combined companies greater than the sum of the two parts. The success of a merger or acquisition depends on whether this synergy is achieved, and we will tackle the subject of synergy realization in a later chapter.

There are many kinds of integration, depending largely on the structure of the acquisition deal. Exhibit 2.1 provides an at-a-glance summary of the most common types of integrations and the projected level of integration support required.

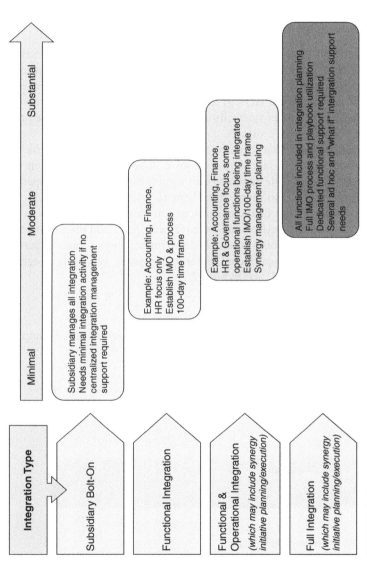

Integration Type

Subsidiary Bolt-On

Minimal / Moderate / Substantial

Subsidiary manages all integration
Needs minimal integration activity if no
centralized integration management
support required

Functional Integration

Example: Accounting, Finance,
HR focus only
Establish IMO & process
100-day time frame

**Functional &
Operational Integration**
*(which may include synergy
initiative planning/execution)*

Example: Accounting, Finance,
HR & Governance focus, some
operational functions being integrated
Establish IMO/100-day time frame
Synergy management planning

Full Integration
*(which may include synergy
initiative planning/execution)*

All functions included in integration planning
Full IMO process and playbook utilization
Dedicated functional support required
Several ad hoc and "what if" intergration support
needs

EXHIBIT 2.1 Integration Support Model Options

The following is a brief explanation of each. Keep in mind that the specific type of integration is dictated by the terms of the deal, and terminology can vary from company to company.

Subsidiary Bolt-on Acquisition

A subsidiary bolt-on acquisition (also called a tuck-in) typically refers to a deal in which a product or company acquisition fits naturally within the buyer's existing business lines or strategy. This is especially prevalent in the private equity realm and refers to a case in which a private equity–backed company acquires another vertically aligned company to enhance the private equity–backed company's value.

In my experience, this scenario requires the least amount of true integration support, and in fact it may require none. The management team typically keeps most of the acquired unit's management team and operation structure largely intact, so there's very little to integrate.

For example, a large financial services company may conduct a bolt-on acquisition in which it buys a small research company and then transfers all of its resources into its own research department. In this case, other than the physical moving of the affected research personnel, very little integration support would be needed. See Exhibit 2.2.

Functional Integration

A functional integration typically occurs with large multinational companies with diversified portfolios of businesses.

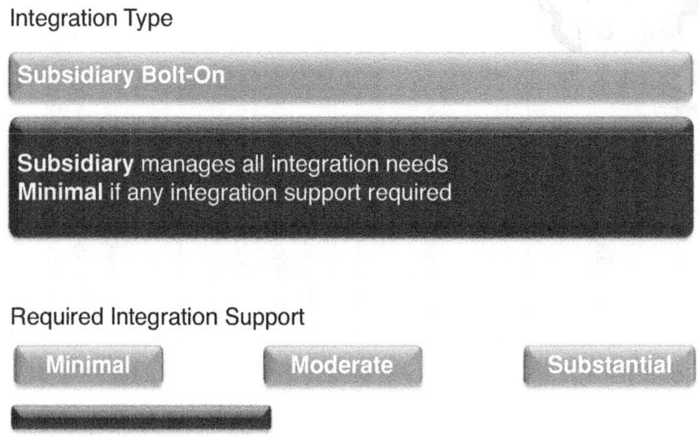

Integration Type

Subsidiary Bolt-On

Subsidiary manages all integration needs
Minimal if any integration support required

Required Integration Support

Minimal   Moderate   Substantial

EXHIBIT 2.2   Subsidiary Bolt-on Support Model

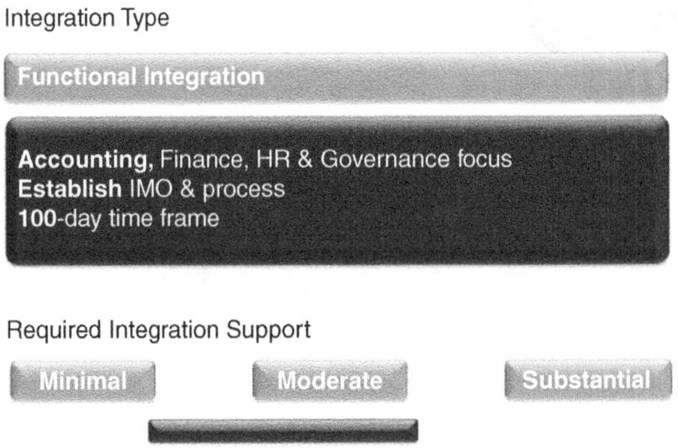

Integration Type

EXHIBIT 2.3   Functional Integration Support Model

In a functional integration, companies integrate key operating functions like human resources (HR), accounting, and legal services but leave the rest of the business largely intact. This type of integration gives the acquirer sufficient control over the new unit in centralized functions like HR and accounting, but typically the acquired company's management team is left intact to manage day-to-day operations.

This type of integration requires integration support, but the amount required and the timing of the integration project will usually be shorter than that of a full integration.

If the functions to be integrated include more departments than HR, accounting, and legal services, this will require more resources and should be treated more like a full operational integration. See Exhibit 2.3.

Functional, Operational, and Full Integrations

Functional, operational, and full integrations involve a specified change in control and typically include senior management changes or restructuring. They are deals in which the operations and headquarters of the acquired company are destined to be moved or closed as part of the arrangement and require a healthy level of integration support, which we will discuss in later chapters. See Exhibit 2.4.

ASSESSING INTEGRATION COMPLEXITY AND RISK

Given all of the complexities involved in actually closing a deal, it is often difficult to think critically about integration. However, you can begin to

Integration Type

> **Functional & Operational Integration**
>
> **Accounting,** Finance, HR & Governance focus
> **Establish** IMO & process
> **Synergy** management planning
> 100-day time frame

Required Integration Support

| Minimal | Moderate | Substantial |

EXHIBIT 2.4   Functional and Operational Support Model

scope the integration challenge early by simply determining what kind of deal is being made. ("Early" can be defined as 60–90 days prior to close.) This will help you to build the business and operational case for integration support and to begin to collect the necessary data to build your integration plan.

It also gives you a head start for securing additional integration resources (whether outside resources or an in-house team) well before your scheduled day one. Day one is when the deal closes and becomes official and is communicated to various stakeholder audiences (e.g., stockholders, employees, and government contacts).

There are many things that are difficult to project or estimate when establishing an integration plan. There's so much in play that divining a clear view of the end state can be quite daunting. Executives are mainly concerned about the following areas:

- Future financial performance
- Future operational performance
- Potential cultural risks
- Potential business risks
- Customer and employee retention

The rest of this chapter deals with some methods to narrow the risk and to inform your integration planning.

After you've gotten a better understanding of the integration type, it is always prudent to do some assessment work to discover what the integration risks are and to gain some understanding of their complexity. This can be accomplished and informed with the following methods:

- A review of due diligence materials (more on that in Chapter 6).
- A series of stakeholder interviews with key executives.
- An analysis of previous integration activities and their successes and failures.

Let's look at each area to get a better understanding of what information can help you to diagnose integration complexity.

Due Diligence

The due diligence list included in Chapter 6 is exhaustive and will, I hope, be more than you need. However, it's advisable to have more information than less, so always ask for more than what you think you need.

After reviewing the materials, some integration complexity clues might arise from the availability of documents. Are the documents any of the following:

- Hard to access?
- Organized well?
- Complete and thorough?

The degree to which due diligence requests for documents are taken care of might be an early clue to the extra work that will be required to fully understand the integration needs and challenges. If there isn't a good level of due diligence, you may be forced to venture out and do your own discovery to get the information you need. A helpful hint is to get the request in as early as possible so you can determine whether this is a problem and whether you will need more time for discovery.

Stakeholder Interviews and Complexity

Another way to attain some risk assessment and complexity guidance is to talk to company executives who are engaged in the merger or acquisition. They will typically provide solid information that can be used to shape your integration strategy.

The optimal integration-risk survey should be created to address the specific company, industry, and deal type for your integration. The following is a list of universal risk-assessment questions you can use to craft your own assessment survey:

- What are the business rationales and the key financial measurements that support the deal?
- What are the core business strategies of the newly combined company (newco) or the acquiring company?*
- What are the most sensitive areas of the business that might be prone to disruption?
- Are there significant government and/or regulatory challenges for this industry (e.g., pharmaceutical integrations)?
- Will some portion or unit of the acquired or merged company be carved out and left alone, making extra effort necessary to preserve it during the integration?
- What are the time-line expectations for the integration that have been communicated to key stakeholder audiences (e.g., the investor community)?
- Are major IT system integrations required to realize synergy benefits or operational efficiency? What are their expected timing?
- Are there any key executives who might leave as a result of the merger or acquisition and create an experience vacuum in a particular area?
- How involved will the integration team be in synergy work-stream tracking and management? (There will be more on this in later chapters, but this is a good detail to consider early.)
- Are there any Environmental Protection Agency (EPA) or union concerns that have to be addressed other than the usual ones?
- Are there any past business practices that are incongruent with the newco's (or the acquiring company's) business strategies (e.g., credit standards for new customers)?
- Are there any community issues that will result in a more rigorous communication plan being required?

These are just samples of the kinds of discovery needed to gauge integration complexity. In addition, you should ask questions that are germane to the industry, the deal type, and the company.

Newco is a commonly used term to refer to a newly merged organization. It can be used to refer to an actual new company (a new initial public offering and stock) or to a newly forming organization. For instance, if two companies are merging, and they keep the acquiring company's name because so much is in flux and being formed, the term *newco* can be used during integration planning and execution.

Stakeholder Interviews and Risk

The degree of risk is a rather subjective premise, and executives will assess it differently based on their tolerance. Much as investment managers assess your personal investment risk profile before investing your money, you should do the same to guide your integration planning.

Your integration-risk survey questions should include questions specific to your particular industry, deal type, and companies. The following are some typical questions to get you started:

- What is the overall business environment for the industry of the merged companies or the acquired companies?
- Are the newly merged companies within close physical proximity (driving distance) or geographically spread out?
- Have the newly merged companies been competitors or did they have a manufacturer-supplier relationship?
- How are the executives defining integration, and what are their expectations of the degree of effort required to integrate the two companies?
- Is the merger or acquisition perceived as a positive development in both organizations, or is there resistance somewhere?
- What is the degree of integration expertise in the organization, and are there key executives with past integration expertise?
- What are the biggest cultural or change management concerns, and does the newco or the acquiring company have any experience in these areas?
- Are there other significant business demands and/or financial pressures on the organization that have the potential to distract from the integration activity?
- Are there significant retention risks for key executives or acquired employees? Are there any plans under way to address this?
- Has the newco senior-executive organizational design been finalized, or has a date for when this will be finalized been communicated? Is there a target date?
- Is there any significant litigation under way that may affect integration planning or timing?

Operating-Style Risk

Every company operates differently, which affects the way the employees behave and manage the business. This is a highly subjective area, but it's advisable to understand some of the differences so you can factor them into your integration planning.

The following are some sample questions that can be integrated into your stakeholder interviews (to be expanded to address industry, deal type, and company-specific issues):

- How have the two companies traditionally approached the markets they serve or operate in? Are they community pillars or more passive in their approach to community affairs?
- How are important decisions made in the organizations? Is one company more top-down and autocratic while the other has more of a bottom-up, consensus-building approach?
- How do people advance in each organization? Is there a tried-and-true path to the top in one company (e.g., through sales) but another path in the other company (e.g., through finance?)
- Are the organization structures well-defined in one company and more informal (e.g., dotted-line or virtual reporting structures) in the other?
- Does one company expect the employees to be on-site all of the time while the other has a telecommuting policy?
- How is information communicated in each company? Does one company do more brown-bag lunches with senior executives while the other does webcasts or memos?
- How do connective-tissue functions like HR, finance, and IT differ in each organization? Does finance call the shots in one organization more than in the other?
- How is spending approved in one company versus the other? Is one more liberal on spending limits than the other?
- How do the companies differ in their approaches to decision making? Does one company tend to overanalyze while the other is more expedient, perhaps relying more on gut experience and intuition than on heavy amounts of research and data?
- Does one company have detailed and current information on its consumer and/or business-to-business segments while the other has less?
- Does one company have more of a nine-to-five style while the other company has more of a norm of working late?

The Evaluation and Measurement of Performance

Another huge operating difference you will need to assess is how performance is evaluated and measured. Although this is typically a work stream that is addressed in HR integration planning, understanding the differences up front can help you to gain a better understanding of many risk and complexity factors.

Here's a sample of the key differences to evaluate between the two companies:

- Is there a standardized performance-management program?
- What is the process for evaluation (direct-line management, 360 review, peer review, or all of these)?
- How often are the employees evaluated (monthly, quarterly, annually)?
- What are the rewards for exceptional performance? How are they administered?
- What are the consequences for poor performance?

Diagnosing significant differences here will help in many ways, including the following:

- Providing the integration team with information to help inform and shape the overall integration plan and strategy.
- Helping the HR integration leaders to understand the challenges of integrating the performance-management programs of the two organizations.
- Helping the creation of cultural and talent assessment tools.

CHAPTER CHECKLIST

After reading this chapter, keep these things on your integration checklist:

Integration Type and Level of Support

- ☐ Determine the integration scope.
- ☐ Determine the integration type.
- ☐ Estimate the amount of integration support required.

Complexity and Risk

- ☐ Review due diligence documents and assess completeness.
- ☐ Complete stakeholder interviews to gauge integration complexity.
- ☐ Complete stakeholder interviews to gauge integration risk.
- ☐ Assess operating-style risk.

SUMMARY

This chapter offered some M&A basics to help you understand the reasons for mergers and acquisitions. It also provided the information you'll need to assess integration risk up front so you can prepare your integration strategy to address potential issues and tailor your approach accordingly.

Next we will explore why integrations are challenging and why they fail to deliver on planned value and pre-deal expectations.

CHAPTER 3

Making the Business Case for Integration

I n this chapter, you will learn the following:

- Common rationales and reasons for M&A activity.
- The most difficult areas of integration activity.
- The most common causes of integration failure.
- The integration challenge and how to make the business case for integration support.
- Integration success factors.

Completing a merger or an acquisition can take months, if not years. It can be an all-consuming endeavor that tests the resources and stamina of management teams and the legions of consultants and financial advisors involved in the process. It can also be expensive: the acquisition costs, the time and effort expended to complete the deal, and the legal and financial due diligence costs.

M&A activity is somewhat cyclical, and there's plenty of research available on that subject, if you are interested. M&A activity is typically driven by the desire to accomplish some or all of the goals discussed in this chapter.

HOW TO IMPROVE PERFORMANCE

The motivation for M&A activity is that acquiring firms seek improved financial performance and shareholder value. Following are some supporting business benefits that are typically considered to improve financial performance and which will help explain some of the why behind the M&A deals you may be lucky enough to help integrate.

Synergy

Synergy management is a big topic and is touched on later in this book. Synergy generally falls into two main categories: cost savings and revenue enhancements that are enabled by the fact that two companies are now being merged into one. *Enabled* is an important word here, since synergy realization is not automatic. Realizing the full projected value of synergy is usually one of the most challenging integration work streams.

Economy of Scale

Economy of scale means that the combined company can reduce its fixed costs by removing duplicate departments or operations relative to the same revenue stream, thus increasing profit margins. Recently there's been a lot of M&A activity in the health-care sector, driven by the desire to achieve improved economies of scale.

Cross-Selling

Cross-selling is the ability to extend complementary product offerings to existing (as well as new) customers. The company previously could not do this, probably because it was competing with the companies whose products it is now cross-selling. For example, a bank that buys a stockbroker firm can then sell its banking products to the stockbroker's customers, and the broker can sign up the bank's customers for brokerage accounts.

Economy of Scope

Economy of scope assumes that the buyer will absorb a major competitor and thus increase its own market power (by capturing increased market share) to set prices. It will thus gain efficiency in demand-side changes by increasing or decreasing the scope of marketing and distribution or by distributing different types of products to increase revenue and market share.

Taxation

Taxation is rarely the primary rationale for a merger or an acquisition, but taxes certainly factor into any business transaction. Sometimes a profitable company can buy a loss maker to use the target's loss to its own advantage by reducing its tax liability. Rules are in place to limit the ability of profitable companies to shop for loss-making companies, which is why this is not a primary driving motive of M&A activity.

Vertical Integration

Vertical integration occurs when upstream and downstream firms merge (or when one acquires the other).

For example, let's assume a furniture company (downstream firm) wants to vertically integrate by purchasing a timber farm and a processing plant (such as a mill), both upstream firms. The furniture company could engage in vertical integration and control the quantity, cost, and quality of its products' raw materials. This could translate into a cost advantage for the producer and justify a deal to buy and vertically integrate the two companies together.

Product and Service Diversification

Another reason companies acquire other companies is to diversify their product and service portfolios and extend the breadth and depth of the products or services they can offer their customers. Expanding a company's offerings can translate into sales and revenue gains by enabling the company to enter new markets.

Measurement of Merger or Acquisition Success

From a pure business standpoint, the following benchmarks are typically used to measure merger success:

- Cash flow
- Quality of new products and services
- Expansion into new markets
- Revenue of the combined entity
- Share price of the combined entity

THE MOST COMPLEX AREAS

Many surveys and past experience will tell you that the following activities are typically the most difficult in any merger or acquisition:

- Human resource integration
- Sales force integration
- Information technology integration
- Marketing communications
- Accounting and finance

But the most difficult of all is the integration of executive-level leadership. This can be difficult for many reasons: egos, leadership styles, and operating cultures, among others. It is the most difficult because until it is finalized it is hard to really gain traction with an integration and transition to the new.

So when mergers go bad, what's the reason? Every integration is unique, but studies have confirmed a few key reasons mergers underdeliver or fail outright. Here they are:

- *Conflicting goals and strategies.* The main problem here seems to be that companies fail to realize they have conflicting strategies until after the integration process has begun.
- *Poor communication.* This unfortunately is a problem in almost every merger, and the primary reason is always that information and decisions can be slow to develop, so people get anxious as a result. It is imperative that integration managers push communication planning, because senior executives tend to undercommunicate.
- *Conflict, conflict, conflict.* When new management teams can't get along, resolve issues, or plan well together, many things will suffer. Conflict is unavoidable, and a little conflict often produces better results. When conflict results in paralysis and execution dysfunction, however, it can significantly retard integration success.
- *Disparate cultures.* Cultural assessment risk and how to manage cultural integration is addressed elsewhere in this book, but sometimes culture clashes can become so distracting that they can grind integrations to a halt. Culture clashes also make most employees anxious and in many cases downright miserable. This is one of the most important areas to stay on top of in your integration planning.

I'm providing all of this information on the difficulty of integration during M&A because it's hard, and if you don't realize this going in, your chances of a successful integration diminish significantly. Securing post-merger or post-acquisition resources will typically require someone to make the case for utilizing additional outside or dedicated internal resources to complete the integration. In my experience, post-acquisition integration support is often overlooked, underfunded, or an unfortunate combination of both. In order to get ahead of it, you should keep the following in mind:

- The bulk of organizational integration management should commence immediately after day one, or you will be running behind and fixing problems rather than preventing them. (Remember that day one is when the deal closes and there is a change of control and the merger or acquisition is "official.")

■ A wait-and-see attitude puts you and your organizations at a severe disadvantage. You'll end up being reactive instead of proactive. Rather than being effectively positioned to shape circumstances, you'll be in a constant state of playing catch-up.

■ Studies done on customer satisfaction in mergers have shown that customers typically expect merging companies to have the majority of their customer issues resolved within 100 days after the closing. Customers will be pretty tolerant of mistakes, glitches, and bumps up to that time, but after about 100 days they expect things to be business as usual.

MAKING THE BUSINESS CASE FOR INTEGRATION SUPPORT

The track record for successful mergers and acquisitions is not a good one. Consider the following:

■ Over 75 percent are either disappointing or outright failures.
■ 50 percent experience losses of productivity and sales in the first eight months.
■ The majority of managers grade their company's efforts as average or poor.
■ Most integrations greatly exceed their time lines or are never completed.
■ Less than 15 percent of deals produce the expected financial results, and nearly 75 percent fail to earn their cost of capital.
■ 60 percent create no shareholder value at all.

Furthermore, a lack of integration support makes it worse, as the following illustrates:

■ More than 50 percent of all integration efforts fail to deliver their targeted value.
■ The majority of the shortfall is attributable to inadequate merger integration planning and execution.
■ Many companies have become good at doing deals, but integration planning and execution is where value is preserved or eroded.

You can affect your post-merger success by being aware of integration challenges and by taking an active role in addressing them properly. Make sure to remember the following about integration work:

- It's not business as usual.
- It's difficult, complex, risky, and often politically charged.
- It requires a good plan and a rigorous process, along with some strong project management skills to keep things on track.
- Sensitivity to the human issues is also required, along with being able to identify and escalate unforeseen issues quickly.

THE CHALLENGES OF INTEGRATION

You must ensure that the senior leaders in your organization understand the challenges of integration so you can establish the business justification for integration support. Only a few companies are serial acquirers who deal with post-merger or post-acquisition integrations year after year. For most, integrations are infrequent events for which there is little understanding. You must educate leaders on what's involved. See Exhibit 3.1.

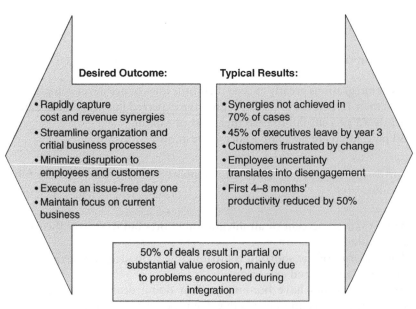

Desired Outcome:

- Rapidly capture cost and revenue synergies
- Streamline organization and critial business processes
- Minimize disruption to employees and customers
- Execute an issue-free day one
- Maintain focus on current business

Typical Results:

- Synergies not achieved in 70% of cases
- 45% of executives leave by year 3
- Customers frustrated by change
- Employee uncertainty translates into disengagement
- First 4–8 months' productivity reduced by 50%

50% of deals result in partial or substantial value erosion, mainly due to problems encountered during integration

EXHIBIT 3.1   Integration Desired Outcomes and Typical Results

Any good executive will outline the risks of a strategic recommendation as well as the risks of doing nothing. The potential pitfalls of poor integration planning include the following:

- Too much focus on getting the deal closed instead of making the deal actually work.
- Too little focus on operational, cultural, strategic, and organizational assessment.
- Overreliance on process and tools and avoidance of the tough issues such as culture and politics.
- No pre-close planning, which puts an integration in catch-up mode right from the start.
- Process driven by activity rather than informed by value preservation, synergy realization, and value creation.
- There is no plan for assigning accountability and tracking for synergy.

These pitfalls happen for a number of reasons, such as the following:

- *Shortchanging the integration effort.* Companies calculate the deal in terms of acquisition cost and benefits and fail to factor integration costs into the mix.
- *Lack of appreciation for integration expertise.* Business integration is treated as just more business as usual. Integration knowledge and experience are not respected as a value creator.
- *Lack of executive "air cover."* A senior executive has not been installed as the champion to own and lead the integration.
- *Overoptimistic benefit realization expectations.* The leadership fully expects the projected benefits to be immediate.

Always remember the bottom line: An acquisition gives you the potential for creating value in the combination, but the business benefits are delivered only in the actual integration. Only 30 percent of the companies doing M&As are successful (as measured by an increase in shareholder value), but the companies that are serious about effective M&A integration have achieved significant and sustainable success, such as 300 percent economic value added (EVA) or a 40 percent increase in stock price.

Also keep in mind that prevention is the best cure. It often helps to model the potential outcomes of poor integration versus the expected results. Synergy projections are often inflated and overly optimistic. Making

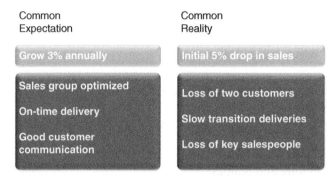

EXHIBIT 3.2 Expectation vs. Reality: Growth
Source: Inchieve, LLC's Financial Impact Calculator

your best case for enhanced integration support may require painting a bleaker picture of the future should sound integration management be lacking.

Exhibits 3.2 through 3.6 address some potential negative outcomes for a chemical company merger.

No one wants to be the one throwing his or her hands up and predicting failure or poor results. The point here is that you will have to fight for integration resources, and you will need to be armed with the facts about why they are important.

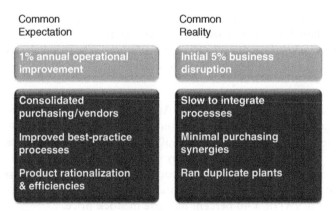

EXHIBIT 3.3 Expectation vs. Reality: Operations
Source: Inchieve, LLC's Financial Impact Calculator

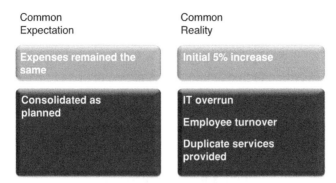

Common
Expectation

Common
Reality

Expenses remained the same

Initial 5% increase

Consolidated as planned

IT overrun

Employee turnover

Duplicate services provided

EXHIBIT 3.4 Expectation vs. Reality: Expenses
Source: Inchieve, LLC's Financial Impact Calculator

A few examples of expectations versus reality can always help to advance the conversation with your senior leadership team. Get serious discussions about integration vetted with your team before it's too late.

Some of the most common poor integration-planning scenarios are the following:

- Failure to achieve all of the strategic advantages that prompted the sponsors to make the deal in the first place, thus wasting the resources that have been devoted to the entire acquisition process.

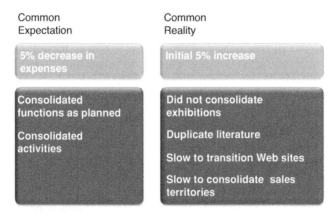

Common
Expectation

Common
Reality

5% decrease in expenses

Initial 5% increase

Consolidated functions as planned

Did not consolidate exhibitions

Consolidated activities

Duplicate literature

Slow to transition Web sites

Slow to consolidate sales territories

EXHIBIT 3.5 Expectation vs. Reality: Expenses
Source: Inchieve, LLC's Financial Impact Calculator

Pretax Op Profit ————— −44%

Net Income ————— −49%

Cash In/Out ————— −50%

Payback ————— +85%

ROI ————— −49%

Company Value ————— −24%

EXHIBIT 3.6   Financial Impact between Common Expectation and Common Reality
Source: Inchieve, LLC's Financial Impact Calculator

- Integration-execution starts that are sloppy and/or inefficient, making it difficult to undo the damage that results.
- A quickly moving competitor who takes advantage of the new organization's inability to respond as a cohesive, well-controlled entity.
- Burnout of the best talent in the newly merged company from being woefully overloaded by the integration distractions.

Exhibit 3.7 illustrates some of the typical challenges of most integrations. When you consider everything that is going on, it's no wonder we see some of the abysmal integration results that are common today.

Integrations can create the perfect storm of business disruption because there is so much going on at once. During an integration, you are trying desperately to capture the synergies that justified the deal in the first place, whether they be personnel reduction, sourcing consolidation, or facilities rationalization.

M&As all have business goals attached to them, as well as a deadline. M&As also integrate two organizations—every function, process, technology, and structure—all at once. As if those two things were not challenging enough, you are also trying to maintain a business-as-usual environment for the affected customers, suppliers, and employees so as not to negatively disrupt the business. Trying to do just one of these things is hard enough. Having to do them concurrently is what makes integration work so difficult to manage.

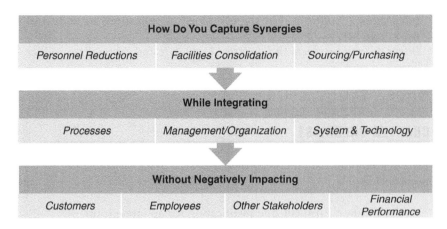

EXHIBIT 3.7 The Integration Challenge

INTEGRATION SUCCESS FACTORS

Post-integration studies and surveys typically point to seven key areas that seem to be common denominators of integration success. When the following areas are done well, integration success seems to follow:

- *Communication.* This should be frequent, positive, and frank at all stages of the integration and with all levels of employees.
- *Establishment of a strong executive management team.* A key area here includes getting the management team in place early and getting the next-level managers in place soon after.
- *Retention of key customers.* Strategies to communicate with the customers before the merger activity is in the news is wise, because your competitors will be calling your customers as soon as they hear the news of your merger.
- *Establishment of a shared vision of the future.* Translate the vision to each division and department so that all the employees know what they need to do.
- *Retention of key employees.* Don't let your top salespeople walk away with your best accounts. You don't want to experience brain drain, because people are an organization's most important assets.

- *Integration of cultures.* Get the combined organizations to unite and work together.
- *Integration of products and services.* Assimilate and rationalize product lines and services.

CHAPTER CHECKLIST

After reading this chapter, keep these research items on your integration checklist:

- ☐ The business rationale and justification for an integration.
- ☐ The most common measures of integration success and what integration areas are most complex.
- ☐ Why integrations underperform or fail.
- ☐ How to make the business case to get integration support.
- ☐ The factors for successful integrations.

SUMMARY

Most integration managers will find themselves, at some point, justifying the level of effort required to manage an integration. Sometimes it is necessary to clearly communicate the challenges and risks of poor integration planning. Be prepared for the challenges, risks, and potential outcomes of poor integration planning so you can educate those around you who may need to be convinced that this is so important.

The next chapter offers some fundamental elements of integration-planning techniques to help you break the task at hand into manageable phases.

CHAPTER 4

An Introduction to Integration Planning

In this chapter, you will learn the following:

- How to break down your integration into manageable phases for planning and execution purposes.
- What factors to consider as you develop timing parameters for your integration project.
- The importance of business vision and strategy in laying the foundation for successful integration planning.
- How to assess the need for external integration help and what to look for in evaluating firms and resources.

As previously mentioned, the purpose of this handbook is to provide a workable approach to integration to fit most scenarios. This chapter offers you the five key stages of the integration life cycle.

Some integrations may require that you break down the five stages into further categories, depending on the complexity of the assignment, but the five stages will provide a good start for any integration team.

Timing is also variable, since some integrations require more time than others. A good basic rule is to try to accomplish the bulk of the integration activity within 120 days, or sooner, if possible, because integrations are hard work and can be a distraction from day-to-day operations. Integration planners should have a strong bias for urgency: a desire to get tasks accomplished on time, or sooner, if possible.

Because of the intensity of most integrations, the 120-day guideline serves to prevent integration fatigue, which occurs when the day-to-day grind of the integration carries on too long and the teams and employees become bored or inattentive. Even worse, integrations that drag on too long risk the loss of key integration managers, who get pulled into more pressing assignments.

A short-staffed and exhausted integration team will make mistakes that can erode the synergies and disrupt operations. Therefore, work smart but fast and complete your integration quickly.

INTEGRATION ACTIVITIES

The bulk of integration activities should be organized into the macro phases in the following list. Chapters 5 through 9 include detailed expositions of each phase. Included here are a few highlights of the activities that each phase entails:

1. *Pre-planning.* Setting the parameters of integration timing, addressing core business strategy issues, if necessary, and securing outside resources.
2. *Integration due diligence.* Securing background data on all functional business areas and business activity to inform your integration planning. An extensive list of typical due diligence materials is included in Chapter 6.
3. *Integration office planning.* Establishing an IMO to run your integration project.
4. *Execution.* All major integration activities, commencing from day one of your integration to end state, which is the official conclusion of the bulk of integration activities.
5. *End state or wrap-up.* Post-integration surveys and integration-closing activities.

INTEGRATION TIMING

Before we get into the typical phases of an integration, let us explore a question often asked in relation to integration planning: How long should this take? The answer depends on many factors, but for most activities the work plans should be accomplished as quickly as possible and the integration completed as soon as possible.

However, some things take longer. Here are some factors to consider as you establish the timing parameters for your integration.

Operations Consolidations

Integrations often require the rationalization of plants or operating facilities, which may take longer to close down than the other work streams of an integration. Closing a plant too quickly can disrupt operations and/or alarm customers and suppliers.

Plan any facility closing carefully to make sure that nothing is done too quickly; this is one of those activities for which it may be prudent to extend the time frame past your typical integration window.

Also, be mindful when dealing with any unionized organizations, whether it's the full employee base or a specialized union. Negotiating changes to any union contracts requires time and careful planning. Be sure to include subject-matter experts in the process.

Pending Acquisitions

Sometimes one acquisition is followed by another, and it may make sense to hold the consolidation of certain functions until all of the acquired entities are closed. For example, if the acquisition of a subsidiary is followed by another acquisition of a similar industry of a similar size, it may make sense to hold any head-count rationalization and organizational planning so you can select candidates from the combined pool of talent.

Information Systems

Integration of IT systems can be a time-intensive process that takes longer to accomplish; it may extend 18–24 months past closing This is acceptable in most cases, because trying to do this too quickly can create system issues that affect many other parts of the organization. One thing you don't need when you are trying to integrate is system instability, so trust your IT professionals to prescribe a timetable that ensures continuity and stability, then factor that timetable into your integration planning.

The honest answer to how long an integration should take is "It depends." However, plan with a bias for urgency and rely on subject-matter experts in the areas just outlined to specify the ideal integration timetable for particular functions and/or work streams.

INTEGRATION AND BUSINESS PLANNING

After you account for the most important facets of your integration planning, it is always prudent to establish an operating vision to guide and shape your planning efforts. Doing so also helps to focus attention on any areas of the overall operating strategy that may still be undefined or in development.

If the newco business strategy is incomplete, it will adversely affect the integration, because people revert to what they know, which may be in conflict with the new organization's goals and objectives.

If you sense that the new business strategy lacks refinement or definition, you are advised to push back until you get it. If you have strategic planning skills, jump in and help to formulate the newco strategy so you can begin your planning work in earnest.

Companies typically overestimate the level of agreement within the organization on the future direction and business strategy of the newly combined organization. This makes setting the vision and strategy for the future organization all the more critical.

Vision and Strategy

It is important to carefully consider the vision and strategy, because a poorly defined business strategy impedes integration planning and causes many problems down the road. As an integration leader, you will sometimes be forced to help the organization clarify important strategy and business-model issues so you can tailor your integration plan to align with the newco's business strategy and operating principles. Here are the key areas that must be well-defined before the integration work gets under way in earnest:

- Full understanding of the business models of both the new and acquired companies.
- Senior executive alignment in both companies.
- The role of boards and sponsoring organizations in governance.
- Operating model principles, as well as functional operating models consistent with the overall operating model.
- The strategy for the transaction and integration.

Delivering Value (and Not Losing Any)

Delivering value is the most critical outcome of any integration. Here are some of the top areas where integration leaders must contribute to the newco's bottom line:

- *Delivery and implementation of the business plan.* Are you establishing an integration plan that aligns with the operating plans of the new organization?
- *Identification and delivery of synergy plan.* Have you created or are you supporting synergy tracking and benefits realization as part of your integration plan? (More on this in Chapter 13.)

- *Attainment of quick-win cost-reduction and revenue-enhancement initiatives.* Have you singled out areas where cost savings and other business benefits can be quickly realized as a result of expedient and sound integration planning and execution?
- *A framework for benefit tracking.* Do you have the tools set up to accurately track and manage the integration synergy plan? (Again, more on this in Chapter 13.)

Managing the Change, People, and Potential Business Disruption

Integrations by nature are one of the most disruptive business events a company and its employees will ever experience. Make sure you assess the people side of an integration and factor it into your planning. The key areas here are the following:

- A retention plan for top talent and/or sales force employees. Make sure your top talent and/or salespeople have a reason to stay.
- A customer retention plan. Don't lose your top customers!
- Organization design, people selection, and timing for the completed organization (when all levels of employees are named).
- Clear reporting lines. Avoid vague or undefined reporting relationships, which are a common quick fix in integration that seldom work.
- A short-term IMO and supporting resources. Make sure you have the resources you need to execute your integration.

INTEGRATION SUPPORT

Based on your level of need and some of the challenges described in this chapter, you may need some outside help. There are many consulting firms that offer integration-related services. Shop around and get recommendations from colleagues and business associates who have some previous integration experience on what firms might be right for your integration.

If you decide to hire short-term consulting support to assist with your integration, here are some things to consider.

Transaction Advisors

Many large consulting firms on transactions also have integration support services. Check with the firm that is helping you with your deal to see if it offers integration support. If it has been involved with your firm for a while, it may have already pitched integration support, but check anyway. Make sure that the integration support is staffed by experienced professionals, and negotiate reasonable rates for a specified time frame.

Specialty Firms

There are many smaller consulting firms that specialize in integration with seasoned professionals with lots of deal experience. This may be the more economical route (though not always, of course), and you're apt to get a more intense level of service from senior-level advisors at a firm like this than you would from a partner-level individual at a large consulting firm. Proceed with an open mind and consider all of your options, because every situation and firm is different.

If the chemistry with the people you'll be working with is acceptable, there are a few other items you will want to check as you consider firms to help you with your integration, including the following.

Firm Experience

- What previous integrations has the firm done? Has it done a variety of integration work (mergers, acquisitions, or bolt-ons)? What is the average deal size for its previous engagements?
- Does it come with recommendations? It's always a good idea to check references to see how past integrations were managed and if the previous clients were pleased with the outcomes.

Client Partner Experience

- Does the firm have managers who have been doers and who have worked in organizations before? Sometimes getting a professional lifelong consultant can help tremendously with the thinking but be less helpful in the doing.
- There's a lot of doing in integration work, to say the least, so ask the person who is going to run your engagement the following: "What have you managed directly before in the corporate world?"

Proven Integration Methodologies

- What tools, practices, and approaches has the firm developed, and what is the track record of those assets in its previous integration work?

Bonus Areas

- Take a look at a firm's integration-thought leadership assets, including articles, publications, surveys, and studies. Firms that have leadership assets focused on thinking about integration are worthy of strong consideration.

■ Make sure the firm is independent. Ideally, you may want to avoid having your integration firm tethered to other major work streams like auditing or IT consolidations.

■ Make sure the firm has experience with integration tools. There are several integration project-management tools available to help with complex integrations. If you are planning to use one, hiring a firm with working knowledge of the tool is advisable.

CHAPTER CHECKLIST

Here are some things to keep in mind while you are engaged in planning your integration:

▢ Break down your integration into manageable phases.
▢ Create a timing parameter for each phase after you have considered mitigating factors such as operations considerations, IT, and any additional acquisition activity your company may be considering.
▢ Make sure the newco business strategy is articulated in a manner that can inform and enhance your integration planning.
▢ Evaluate the need for additional integration resources to support your activities.

SUMMARY

This chapter provided some basic pre-planning activities you can undertake to understand the what and the how of managing your integration.

Next we will explore some more specific activities you should undertake as part of the official integration pre-planning phase.

CHAPTER **5**

The Pre-Planning Phase

I n this chapter, you will learn the following:

* The most common key activities that are part of integration pre-planning.
* How to stress-test the synergy plan.
* What to look for in your due diligence assessments.
* Assessing potential challenge areas like culture and change management.

The pre-planning phase should begin as soon as a deal is imminent and a target closing date has been set. This is when companies typically make decisions to seek outside external support to augment their integration teams or to handle the integration internally. Either way, this is when it is critical to access the integration challenge and determine what resources will be required to manage it.

Deal teams are typically reticent to allow too much pre-deal integration planning, since they are focused on closing the deal (which they should be). However, this is when those executives tasked with integration should have sharp elbows and get involved in the conversation to begin planning. Even if the integration details are a bit thin, getting involved before the deal is closed will accelerate your planning and integration preparation.

KEY ACTIVITIES

In some cases, integration teams have been involved early to stress-test some initial synergy projections and assumptions. This reality test often results in some much-needed tweaks to the deal specifics that lead to smoother integrations post-closing. There are a number of key activities, described here.

Determining Integration Type

As outlined in an earlier chapter, there are several common integration types, and determining whether the integration is a subsidiary bolt-on or a functional and operational integration, for example, is a key planning detail.

Agreeing on this up front will ensure that senior management is aligned on the type of integration, which will make subsequent planning much easier.

Stress Testing and Synergy Assumptions

Having access to deal information is not always possible, so this activity is largely dependent on how much information is available, when it is available, and to whom.

If you are fortunate to have access to some of the deal details and can provide feedback, it can help in proper integration planning by providing the deal team with important feedback that it can consider in its terms.

Here are some key things to look for:

- *Timing.* Are integration timetables referenced, and are they realistic?
- *Integration support.* Is the proper expectation being set for the amount of integration support required? Has the cost been estimated and addressed? Note that integration costs are often included in the acquisition cost detail.
- *Synergy realities.* Are there some synergy scenarios and projections that are too optimistic and need a reality check? For example, if you are working on a chemical company integration in which the plant consolidation time lines are substantially underestimated because of the extended closing time frames dictated by EPA regulations, consider this in the analysis.
- *Estimated closing date.* Closing dates can sometimes be a moving target, but there is often a target date you can establish for your integration planning.

REVIEWING THE PLANNING DOCUMENTS

Access to due diligence documents can provide a wealth of information for your integration efforts. You should make sure you get access and have the time to digest this content before finalizing your integration plans. Here's a small sample of information you might find in a typical "clean room."*

---

*The term *clean room* is used to describe a neutral environment where information can be securely shared between parties that are planning an acquisition or integration. Today most clean rooms are virtual datasites where information can be loaded and accessed only by approved personnel.

Labor

Labor unions require specialized treatment for integration planning, and the existence of unions in the acquired labor force is a good thing to know about in advance. Becoming familiar with the collective bargaining agreement of the union before beginning any workforce consolidation efforts is a must.

It's also important to keep in mind that any labor planning that involves a union should include someone from the HR department and sometimes even someone from legal services. Labor contracts can be terribly complex, so reach out to the subject-matter experts early in your planning, and communicate often in dealing with unions.

Employee Data

Since you might have position duplication, getting access to past performance reviews can jump-start the talent assessment process, so decision makers down the road can make the best choices for staffing. Getting these data organized for them can speed up their processes and give them the information they need to make fair, unbiased talent decisions to finalize their organizations.

Store and Plant Data

An integration may require the need to close duplicative retail stores and/or plants when two companies merge. Getting access to productivity data can help integration managers to build rationalization models to inform closing decisions and time frames. Plant and/or facility rationalizations (i.e., closings) can be an important element of an acquisition strategy because they present an opportunity for significant synergies. Plant rationalizations can, for example, support efforts to increase the scale of a company's manufacturing facilities and reduce its fixed-cost base.

Remember that closing anything after integration can be an emotional exercise, since it usually involves job losses. Integration managers can make this process objective and unbiased by gathering all necessary information and building the proper models to help the deal's decision makers make solid, informed decisions that are grounded in fact and easy to communicate to the stakeholder communities.

Stakeholder Communities or Audiences

Another output of clean-room planning is a good understanding of all the various stakeholder audiences that have to be accounted for in communication planning for integration. Stakeholders are defined as any audience affected by integration, specifically the following:

- Employees
- Shareholders
- Suppliers
- Customers
- The investment community (e.g., analysts)
- The local community (the geographic area where a company operates)

Integration managers should make a short list of all the audiences that will require outreach during the integration.

ASSESSING POTENTIAL CHALLENGE AREAS

After you've collected and analyzed the pre-planning information referenced here, assess the potential integration risks and challenges at a high level to see if you are missing any important areas. Below is a collection of typical hot spots to consider, as well as some questions to ask as you prepare.

Effective Plan Management and Governance

When you assess the challenging areas, be sure to review the program management and governance of your integration plan. Questions should include the following:

- What is the right governance structure for the integration plan you are implementing?
- Do you have the capabilities and resources required to execute your plan well?
- Are you prepared to implement your integration plan based on the expected day-one timing?

Delivering Value

Integrations have to deliver on the expected value. It is easy to erode value with poor integration planning and execution. *Value* is typically defined as the aggregate business benefit derived from cost saving, revenue enhancement, and operating efficiency. For a merger and/or an acquisition to make financial sense, it has to provide business benefits that can be forecasted and that provide the justification for the deal. No corporate board is going to sign off on a merger unless it delivers tangible business value that can be realized within a specified time frame.

As you assess your plan's ability to deliver in this area, ask the following questions:

- How can value be delivered with the challenges you are forecasting in terms of people, culture, and continuing business?
- How can you mitigate adverse disruptions in day-to-day operations during integration?
- Are your synergy targets realistic? Is the collective buy-in from senior management attainable?
- What changes may be necessary in the operating model to ensure a successful integration?
- Is the timing for synergy realization realistic?

Establishing the Right Level of Integration

When reviewing your plan and the value expectations, consider the following:

- What is the right level of integration to deliver value and attain business objectives?
- What is the recommended pace and timetable for your integration? Is it too short or too long when weighed with other considerations? Are there integration decisions that have to be delayed for some reason?
- Do you have the right level of resources (internal and external) to manage the integration activity?

Culture in a Business Environment

Culture is the force that helps to shape what people in an organization think, how they behave and interact with one another, and what they value. When the cultures in two organizations differ, even a little, it can create dysfunction that can retard the achievement of the desired end state, and at its worst it adversely affect business results. When people can't work together well, business tends to suffer.

When reviewing your challenges, consider the following questions about culture in a business environment:

- What are the most prevalent cultural differences between the two companies that are integrating? What might happen if the cultural differences are not addressed?

- How much cultural integration work will be required as part of the integration's planning and execution?
- How are you going to manage the sometimes conflicting needs of all of the stakeholders?
- How will you ensure that communication is frequent and relevant and adds value to all the stakeholder audiences?
- What are the normal pressures of the integration on the culture's day-to-day operations?
- What potentially adverse or disruptive events could threaten normal operations during the integration?
- Are there any political or environmental issues that could distract from the integration planning and execution?

We'll discuss cultural change in more detail later in this book, but keep in mind that it may be one of the most written-about business topics because when there are cultural clashes in a company (or between two companies in an integration), it can be a destructive force.

There are some fabulous thought leaders in the area of cultural integration, so if you think you have a storm brewing in this area, seek out one of these leaders early and get advice. For instance, Price Pritchett is a consultant who has written several books on the subject and is considered the foremost expert on it. I highly recommend that you visit www.pritchettnet.com for more guidance on managing cultural change if you think it's going to be an especially challenging area of your integration.

A few things that make up an organization's cultural DNA are the following:

- *Behavior.* What types of activities are performed and rewarded? What types are shunned?
- *Functions.* How are people organized? How do they get things done?
- *Rules.* What are the rules and how are they enforced?
- *Organizational structure.* How are the people in a department or a company organized, and what are the policies and processes that dictate the ways they work together?
- *Symbols.* What legacy images, people, or assets have special meaning, and why?
- *History.* What elements of the company's history have significant meaning and value to the employees?
- *Traditions.* What historical events and stories are held in esteem by the collective organization?

We discuss the topic of cultural integration as part of an integration plan later in this book, but for now, being aware of the degree of cultural differences is critical as you complete your integration pre-planning.

CHAPTER CHECKLIST

Keep in mind the following pre-planning activities and research:

☐ Determine the integration type.
☐ Do some stress testing and be aware of synergy assumptions.
☐ Make sure to review the planning documents.
☐ Assess potential challenge areas.
☐ Assess the kinds of cultural changes that are required in your integration.

SUMMARY

In this chapter, we reviewed some of the most important areas to analyze as part of integration pre-planning. Time spent here will make execution easier, and it will save you time in the long run, in most cases. Make sure you allow a fair amount of time at the start of integration for pre-planning.

Next we will review a comprehensive list of typical due diligence information you should consider as you prepare for your integration.

CHAPTER 6

The Importance of Due Diligence

In this chapter, you will learn the following:

- The goals for the due diligence phase of integration planning.
- A summary of the numerous documents you should consider for your due diligence assessment.

Due diligence officially occurs prior to closing (although sometimes key activities can occur after closing, but that's not preferable). In the due diligence phase, integration leaders need to be highly engaged and preparing for the deal to close in anticipation of the integration's official starting date.

In large mergers and acquisitions, the due diligence phase may necessitate the creation of a virtual datasite, or clean room, for the housing of sensitive documents crucial to the deal's integration planning. Access to such a clean room would be restricted, minimizing security breaches during this critical phase so there is no margin of error.

As mentioned in the preceding chapter, a clean room is a secure space where all the applicable data for the integration is housed. Creating a clean room is one of two main methods of accomplishing document security in integration. The clean room is a place where the integration's data are set up and monitored by security and where investors and other interested parties can spend hours, one group at a time, reviewing all the pertinent information.

The other main method of facilitating due diligence, and the better one, is the process by which companies establish a virtual dataroom (VDR). The VDR takes the antiquated concept of a physical dataroom and makes the information available in a secure electronic environment instead.

VDR solutions are the norm for most mergers these days. In fact, there are several varieties of VDR applications on the market. Exploring the VDR solutions options at the beginning of your due diligence process is a must so that data can be stored and exchanged during the integration without security concerns.

As you might guess, acquiring the most important and pertinent information in an integration is an important activity. The most common types of information needs for integration are listed below. Integration managers should avoid dumping this list on just one participant, because the gathering process can be time-consuming and a distraction from the daily needs of a business. Instead, prioritizing the data collection needs and spreading out the request over several weeks can help to avoid a situation in which the employees are overloaded.

Overall, the key goals in good data collection include the following:

- Understanding the key aspects of the target company's organization, governance, and business processes.
- Collecting inputs to support the development of the initial integration plan.
- Mitigating duplicate data requests to a target company and allowing the due diligence team to stay focused on the aspects of a deal's closing.

Remember not to inundate the deal team with requests for information you may not need. "I'll take whatever you've got" is a sure way to get nothing. Exhaustive requests irritate transaction personnel, who are most likely very busy trying to close the deal. Ask only for what you really need, based on your pre-planning activities.

DUE DILIGENCE DOCUMENTS LISTS

There are certain documents that will be necessary to collect for due diligence when you are planning your integration. The lists below outline some of the documents that you would review in connection with integration. The lists are fairly generic and include nearly every piece of information you might need. Note that you will not need all of this information for your integration planning, but this list will give you an idea of the kinds of documentation that may be available. Again, be prudent in your document requests; ask only for what you need.

The items below represent a standard due diligence request list for Company XYZ. It attempts to be overinclusive rather than underinclusive. Not all of them will be appropriate to every integration.

Corporate Books and Records

Corporate books and records can include the following:

- Charter and bylaws
- Minutes of meetings and unanimous written consents

- Officers' and directors' questionnaires
- Shareholder records and reports
- Qualifications and registrations

Charter and Bylaws   The charter and bylaws can include the following:

- The original certificate of incorporation of Company XYZ and all amendments thereto.
- The bylaws of Company XYZ, as amended.
- The charter and bylaws of each wholly or partially owned subsidiary of Company XYZ and of any joint venture involving Company XYZ or its subsidiaries.
- Closing record books for any material corporate transactions, such as the reorganization into a holding company structure or joint ventures.
- Other relevant legal documents governing the organization and management of Company XYZ.

Minutes of Meetings and Unanimous Written Consents   Minutes of meetings and unanimous written consents can include documents created since the date of incorporation of Company XYZ, its subsidiaries, or a joint venture involving Company XYZ or its subsidiaries. Such documents may pertain to the following:

- Shareholders
- Board of directors
- Executive committee
- Audit committee
- Any other committees
- Specific authorizing resolutions
- Material (including financial projections), distributed to the board of directors or any committees in connection with the most recent meetings of the board or committees.

Shareholder Records and Reports   Shareholders records can include the following:

- The shareholder list and other stock records.
- Shareholder agreements, voting trusts, proxy agreements, escrow agreements, or similar arrangements.
- Stock purchase agreements with the shareholders.
- Agreements relating to preemptive rights or other preferential rights of the shareholders.
- Agreements restricting the sale or other disposition of capital stock.

- Agreements or plans concerning outstanding or proposed stock options, warrants, or rights, including employee stock-ownership plans.
- Agreements relating to the registration rights of the shareholders.
- Trust agreements or other documents for shares held in a fiduciary capacity.
- Annual reports.
- Quarterly and special interim reports since the most recent annual report.

Qualifications and Registrations   Qualifications and registrations can include the following:

- A list of jurisdictions where Company XYZ is qualified as a foreign corporation or is licensed to do business.
- Any other material governmental qualifications, registrations, business licenses, permits, authorizations, exemptions, or security clearances, including those pursuant to federal or state antitrust, environmental, nuclear regulatory, public utility, public service, or securities laws and regulations.

Financial Information

There are various documents to refer to for financial information on Company XYZ, and these include the following categories:

- Financial statements
- Business plans
- Tax materials
- Indebtedness records
- Miscellaneous

Financial Statements   Financial statements to collect can include the following:

- Consolidated financial statements for all years and interim periods subsequent to the most recent fiscal year end.
- Monthly income statements for the most recent 12 months.
- Internal financial projections (e.g., profit and loss or capital expenditures) and all supporting information.
- A list of off–balance sheet liabilities not appearing in the most recent financial statements (including the notes).
- Auditors' reports (management letters) and management responses.
- Summaries of accounting policies to the extent not disclosed in financial statements.

Business Plans   Business plans to review can include the following:

- Copies of Company XYZ's business or strategic plans.
- Current market strategies that highlight market and brand positions, distinctive competencies, selling capabilities, service, and overall competitive position.
- Company XYZ's visions for growth.

Tax Materials   The various tax materials to collect for Company XYZ can include the following:

- Copies of all federal, state, and municipal tax returns and other filings with tax authorities.
- Copies of all notices of assessment, reassessment, requests for information, and any other related objections or appeals; other documents, including, without limitation, the results of any audit or investigation; closing agreements with all domestic federal, state, local, and foreign taxing authorities for closed years; current examinations by any taxing authorities for closed years; current examinations by any taxing authority; copies of all information requests from, and other correspondence with, the taxing authority pertaining to the year or years under examination.
- Copies of correspondence to and from all domestic federal, state, and local taxing authorities as well as all foreign taxing authorities.
- Copies of all federal, state, and local sales and use tax, value added tax (VAT), and goods and services tax (GST) filings and supporting work papers.
- Analysis of the current and deferred tax provisions and liability accounts up to and including the most recent interim period, including, without limitation, a summary of book and tax timing differences, a reconciliation of the tax provision to the tax returns, including copies of, or access to, the tax provision work papers of Company XYZ's external accountants.
- Copies of any federal or state tax rulings or determination letters, including any withdrawn rulings and letters.
- Details of all transfers to and from reserves with respect to foreign exchange differences.
- Details of any losses carried forward and any other tax attribute carryforwards, including available tax credits, expiration dates, and limitations with respect to their use, along with supporting schedules and other work papers.
- Descriptions of any accounting method changes and copies of all correspondence regarding such method changes.

- Copies of any tax elections made by or on behalf of Company XYZ or its subsidiaries.
- Details of all payroll remittances and other withholdings.
- Copies of all tax-related correspondence to and from Company XYZ's tax advisors.
- Copies of all tax sharing, tax allocation, tax indemnity, and similar agreements.
- Details of any encumbrances for taxes.
- Descriptions of and documentation relating to any pending issues with tax authorities.
- The tax basis of Company XYZ's assets and of its subsidiaries' capital stock and assets.
- Tax sharing or indemnity agreements.
- Closing letters and closing agreements, appeals reports, tax litigation status, Internal Revenue Service (IRS) rulings and technical advice memoranda, and any other material IRS documents and tax assessment documents.

Indebtedness Records   Documents showing indebtedness can include the following:

- All instruments proving debt obligations or lines of credit and all related agreements and material correspondence.
- Any other actual or contingent indebtedness (e.g., loan guarantees, letters of credit, bankers' acceptances, or swaps) not reflected in the most recent financial statements; all related agreements and material correspondence.
- A list of the existing key financing institutions.

Miscellaneous   Various other documents with financial information can include the following:

- Schedules of current notes payable and receivable, intercompany advances, and descriptions of the cash management system.
- Descriptions and lists of current reserves.
- Descriptions of revenue and cost recognition policies.
- Breakdowns of selling, distribution, marketing, and administrative expenses.
- Explanations of foreign exchange accounting policies.
- Information regarding any indebtedness to Company XYZ or to any of its subsidiaries by the directors and senior officers.
- Cost of sales breakdowns.

Employee Materials

The main types of employee materials useful for review in your integration planning can include the following:

- Agreements
- Benefit plans
- Organizational information

Agreements   Agreement documentation can include the following:

- Employment agreements (including, but not limited to, contracts with management personnel or entities affiliated with management personnel).
- Collective bargaining agreements.
- Consulting agreements.
- Employee handbooks, summaries, guidelines, and bulletins.
- Schedules of salaried and hourly employees showing their current compensation rates and breaking down employees by the following:
    - Geographic location
    - Function
    - Age
    - Years with Company XYZ
    - Union versus nonunion
    - Participation in employee benefit plans
    - Part-time versus full-time
- Descriptions of labor disputes, requests for arbitration or mediation, and grievance proceedings.
- Descriptions of negotiations with any unit or group seeking to become the bargaining unit for employees.
- Employee turnover, absentee history, and severance policy.
- Descriptions of any union representation elections.

Benefit Plans   Documentation regarding benefit plans can include the following:

- Pension, supplemental pension, retirement, post-retirement, stock option, severance, incentive, profit-sharing, executive compensation, bonus, and other employee benefit plans (and any related trust agreements and insurance or annuity contracts); information regarding employer stock, a schedule of plan assets, a detailed description of the plan (including structure), and a list of trustees.

- Audit and actuarial studies and reports, including summary plan descriptions, annual returns and IRS filings, pension and retirement plans, and details of any other accrued liabilities.
- Lists of asset transfers or other withdrawals, partial windups, or contribution holidays with respect to all pension plans.

Organizational Information   Documents showing organizational information can include the following:

- Detailed organizational charts.
- A list of all directors and officers.
- Biographies of senior management and any outside directors.
- Schedules showing number of employees for each year and interim periods.
- Lists and descriptions of current operations of each key business unit at Company XYZ showing the following:
  - Business purpose
  - Key manager
  - Key markets served
  - Key facilities

Contingent Liabilities

Documents showing the contingent liabilities of Company XYZ can include the following categories:

- Litigation
- Regulatory compliance

Litigation   Litigation documentation can include the following:

- Lists of all pending or threatened litigation, arbitration, or administrative or other proceedings involving Company XYZ, its subsidiaries, a joint venture involving Company XYZ or its subsidiaries, or any officer or director (including parties, remedies sought, and nature of the action).
- Lists and descriptions of all pending or threatened government or other investigations involving Company XYZ, its subsidiaries, or any officer or director.
- Pleadings and other material documents in material litigation, arbitration, investigations, and other proceedings.

- Consent decrees, judgments, and any other situation in which there are continuing or contingent obligations.
- Letters from lawyers to auditors concerning litigation and other legal proceedings.

Regulatory Compliance Regulatory compliance documentation can include the following:

- Descriptions of any violations of governmental laws or regulations.
- Material reports to governmental agencies.
- Reports, notices, or other correspondence concerning any known or alleged violation of federal or state antitrust, environmental, nuclear regulatory, public utility, public service, or securities laws and regulations.
- Agreements or commitments with governmental entities or other individuals relating to cleanup obligations or other environmental liabilities.
- Copies of correspondence between federal or state government agencies and Company XYZ.
- A list of all governmental filings and consents required for a purchase of the stock of Company XYZ.

Contracts, Agreements, and Other Arrangements

The main types of contracts and agreements for review in your integration planning can include the following:

- Those not found in the ordinary course of business.
- Those found in the ordinary course of business.

Those Not Found in the Ordinary Course of Business Documents not found in the ordinary course of business can include the following:

- Partnership agreements.
- Joint venture agreements.
- Contracts relating to material business acquisitions or dispositions (by transfer of capital stock or assets), including any separate tax or environmental agreements.
- Stand-still agreements.
- Confidentiality and trade-secret agreements.
- Agreements limiting the ability to compete with any other person or to engage in any line of business.
- Corporate transactions with managers, directors, or affiliates.

- Agreements to provide goods or services at below cost (other than promotional arrangements in the ordinary course of business).
- Indemnification agreements for directors and officers.
- Other existing or pending material contracts not in the ordinary course of business.
- Any material correspondence related to the above.
- Closing record books with respect to each transaction.

Those Found in the Ordinary Course of Business   Documents found in the ordinary course of business can include the following:

- A list and descriptions of key customer contracts.
- A list and descriptions of key supply contracts.
- Material sales representative, marketing, agency, or distributorship agreements.
- Material advertising agreements.
- Material government contracts.
- Agreements already made or expected to be made for material capital expenditures.
- Guarantee agreements.
- Agreements that contain change-of-control provisions.
- Any contracts or agreements similar to the above that are presently under negotiation.
- Any material correspondence related to the above.

Proprietary Rights

Proprietary rights documents can include the following:

- Lists and details of any material intellectual property rights that have been registered or for which applications for registration have been filed, including patents, licenses, trademarks, trade names, domain names, copyrights, and other intellectual property rights (including technology transfers).
- The particulars of any license, royalty, and other intellectual property agreements in which Company XYZ, its subsidiaries, or a joint venture involving Company XYZ or its subsidiaries is licensor or licensee.
- Lists and descriptions of any pending or threatened claims for infringement or other violations of proprietary rights owned or used in the business of Company XYZ, its subsidiaries, or a joint venture involving Company XYZ or its subsidiaries, including any challenges as to the validity, subsistence, or ownership of such rights.

- Lists and descriptions of any suspected or alleged infringement by third parties of intellectual property rights owned by Company XYZ, its subsidiaries, or a joint venture involving Company XYZ or its subsidiaries, or used in their business.
- Arrangements for the disclosure of confidential information (which includes technical and commercial information and know-how that is not in the public domain) either by or to Company XYZ, its subsidiaries, or a joint venture involving Company XYZ or its subsidiaries.
- Details of any agreements with employees and consultants regarding their use of the confidential information of Company XYZ, its subsidiaries, or a joint venture involving Company XYZ or its subsidiaries.
- Agreements, policies, or other arrangements relating to the proprietary rights of employees in the products of Company XYZ, its subsidiaries, or a joint venture involving Company XYZ or its subsidiaries (including royalty or other fee arrangements).

Plant, Property, and Equipment

Plant, property, and equipment documents can include the following categories:

- Real property
- Personal property
- Miscellaneous

Real Property   Real property documentation can include the following:

- Descriptions, locations, and character of all real property owned.
- Material deeds, surveys, and other real property-title documents.
- A list of material real property mortgages that are not disclosed in the most recent financial statements.
- A list of all leased real property, including descriptions, terms of leases, sale and leaseback arrangements, options, and annual costs.
- Reporting letters and opinions regarding the acquisition of any material real property.
- A list of title insurance policies.

Personal Property   Personal property documentation can include the following:

- Descriptions, locations, and character of all personal property owned.
- A list of all material leased personal property, including descriptions, terms of leases, options, and annual costs.

Miscellaneous Miscellaneous property documents can include the following:

- Descriptions of facilities and plant, including lists of all material fixed assets and accumulated depreciation.
- Available appraisals.

Insurance

Insurance documents that may be useful in your integration planning can include the following:

- Lists and descriptions of all material property, casualty, liability, and other insurance policies.
- Directors' and officers' liability insurance policies.
- Descriptions of present reserves for, and all potential claims with respect to, any self-insurance.
- Histories of all insured claims, including paid, reserved, and related expense amounts (first dollar loss run).
- Loss runs for workers' compensation and general liability.
- Loss histories for any self-insurance (first dollar loss run).
- Loss prevention or control recommendations made by insurers, brokers, or consultants.

Sales and Marketing

- Descriptions of the markets in which Company XYZ, its subsidiaries, or a joint venture involving Company XYZ or its subsidiaries operate, identifying the type of customers and the size of the overall market (by value).
- Identification details of any customers who account for more than 1 percent of the annual sales of Company XYZ, its subsidiaries, or a joint venture involving Company XYZ or its subsidiaries—or, if there are more than 10 such customers, the 10 largest customers, potentially including the following:
  - The quarterly totals of sales.
  - Details of current sales order statistics available to management.
  - Sales comparison with the industry.
  - Copies of standard sales correspondence, returns, and allowance material along with samples of all forms of purchase orders, invoices, warranty agreements, and guarantees.
  - Details of pricing policies and fluctuations.

- Copies of all printed price lists.
- Identification of principal competitors; a description of the basis of competition and the strength and weaknesses of the principal competitors.
- Indication of the relative size within the industry of Company XYZ, its subsidiaries, or a joint venture involving Company XYZ or its subsidiaries. Details of trade associations relating to the business and any company memberships.
- Details of the current advertising program (including copies of all promotional or other materials used or capable of use in connection with the business) and the cost of this and any other promotion program.
- Details of sales policies and methods of remuneration of sales personnel.
- Policies on product warranties and the rights of customers to refunds, exchanges, or credits after a purchase; the value of refunds, exchanges, or credits given; warranty claims.
- A list of the 10 largest suppliers.
- Current research and development plans and budgets.
- Correspondence and other documents relating to negotiations with competitors of Company XYZ.
- Consulting, engineering, or management reports and marketing studies relating to broad aspects of the business, operations, or products.

Miscellaneous/General Business

Miscellaneous documents for due diligence can include the following:

- Press releases.
- Lists and descriptions of subsidiaries, joint ventures, and partnerships.
- Descriptions of future acquisition or disposition plans.
- Descriptions of future restructuring plans.
- Descriptions of Company XYZ's information management system, including any planned future changes.

A FEW WORDS ABOUT IT DUE DILIGENCE

Thorough analysis of the IT infrastructure at the acquired company is a must. This can be the source of much pain and suffering (i.e., expense and time) down the road if it is not managed well from the start of your integration planning. Chapter 15 addresses proper IT integration, but for now keep in mind the following IT due diligence objectives:

- To understand the current IT portfolio, including application, infrastructure, project, and organization.
- To identify risks for capital needs and opportunities for cost saving related to the IT portfolio's capability to meet current and future business demands.
- To identify risks for capital needs and opportunities for cost saving related to the IT organization's ability to maintain the current and future IT portfolio.
- To identify any gaps relative to specific industry compliance needs and to prepare the remediation plan.

CHAPTER CHECKLIST

Due diligence planning is an important phase of your integration preparations. Remember to do the following:

- ☐ Clarify your data collection goals in preplanning.
- ☐ Ask only for what you need.
- ☐ Always protect and safeguard due diligence documents and follow any protocols that have been established to protect the security of this information.

SUMMARY

The document lists in this chapter are fairly exhaustive and most likely more than you need for your integration. The most important conclusion to draw from this due diligence exercise is to make sure you get access to and analyze as much information as possible so you can inform your integration pre-planning.

Look over these lists and work with your senior management staff to decide on what you really need in terms of documents and information and what is available to review as you plan an integration.

Next we will outline how to establish an IMO to support your organization's integration activity.

CHAPTER 7

Establishing an Integration Management Office

I n this chapter, you will learn the following:

- The rationale for setting up an IMO.
- Various options for support and structure for your IMO.
- How to secure functional resources for your integration.
- How to establish an integration charter and a governance approach for your integration.

Establishing an IMO plan for the purposes of managing integration is highly recommended. It provides a home base for all integration activities and can be set up as a unique cost center to capture integration-related expenses.

In essence, an IMO is a temporary project management office that does the following:

- Drives the development of the overall integration plan, including all of the integration projects, communications plan, and achievements of synergy benefits.
- Defines and manages your integration processes, including functional work-plan reviews, cross-functional collaborations, issue management plans, and executive status updates.
- Manages stakeholder communication, including lists of company executives, functional resource owners, and acquired company management roles.
- Drives the pace of integration.
- Tracks continual improvements, such as measuring and surveying various areas and incorporating feedback into updated integration processes and tools.

The IMO should be established at least 60 days before day one of the integration to allow time for integration-activity scoping, staffing, and securing a physical space to house integration staffers and any consulting or contracting resources that may be engaged for ancillary support.

It is recommended that IMO leaders find some physical office space that they can plant themselves in at both company locations (the acquiring company and the acquired or merged company). This is essential because integration team members will require secure work and collaboration spaces for the duration of the integration.

Most IMO locations can feel like a war room, with lots of whiteboards and wall space for posting materials to support integration activities.

Having some dedicated IMO space allows you to collect a good deal of materials that have to remain confidential and secure. Along with keeping information safer, IMOs can also be used for private discussions about employee issues and other matters that need to be addressed behind closed doors. However, when you're not discussing a confidential matter, it is a good idea to always have your door open, especially when you're at the acquired company's location.

Employees at acquired companies are experiencing an intense level of change, and IMO leaders often become sounding boards for issues, problems, and concerns. Even if you can't fix or even address many of these issues, the fact that you are there and in a responsive mode helps to keep the employees focused on the business. Therefore, it's advisable to be accessible when on-site: Close your laptop to listen when someone comes in to discuss a matter, for instance. By doing so, many times you will uncover potential issues that need attention and that the IMO can address.

One thing to be aware of, however, is that while you have your door open and are available to listen, make sure the IMO office does not become the complaint department. Integrations create disruption and change that affect people in a variety of ways, and some people feel compelled to pinpoint every inconvenience they are experiencing or share their personal thoughts on the perceived problems with the new organization.

As an integration leader, you must solicit constructive criticism and politely but firmly ward off the typical noise of complaints. Once the employees realize the IMO is not a way station for complaints, they will back off. Here are a few tips for addressing complaint issues:

- Always have an open door, but remind people you are soliciting feedback that can help to improve work streams or inform a specific solution.
- Avoid discussing personnel issues that are centered on the inability of two or more people to work well together, because these complaints are usually intended to influence personnel decisions. Personnel decisions

should be made without any bias and undocumented information (i.e., hearsay).

■ If an employee raises a personnel issue that may suggest a conduct or ethical violation, you should engage your HR contact immediately and brief him or her on the issue.

■ Avoid discussions that are centered on an employee's opinion of the company's strategy, executive leadership decisions, or any other high-level issues. These may be interesting discussions, but the employees should be focused on day-to-day operations so as not to disrupt the business any more than it is already being disrupted.

■ If, despite all of these practices, you have an affected employee who is complaining unprofessionally, distracting others, and generally being counterproductive, address the problem quickly. Disgruntled employees are like a cancer in an integration because people are already sensitive. Having someone walking the halls with a bad attitude helps no one. These are typically people who are on their way out, anyway, and if that is actually the case, my recommendation is to execute the separation as soon as allowed by your HR guidelines.

SETTING UP AN IMO

Integration support needs typically vary based on the type of integration you are involved in. The different types of support were outlined in Chapter 2, but the following takes that information and applies it to IMO planning, because knowing how to plan and staff your IMO should be informed by integration type. This will make sure you have the appropriate resources for your integration needs. See Exhibit 7.1.

Verifying Integration Type and the Level of Support Required

IMOs can vary, and there is no hard-and-fast rule for specific organizational structures, number of people, and reporting lines. The best IMO for your integration is one that might do the following:

■ Establish a formal structure with clear roles and responsibilities.
■ Leverage the acquiring and acquired company personnel.
■ Report to a C-level executive.
■ Have a method established to manage integration information, such as project management software SharePoint or Basecamp. (This software provides integration leaders a place to deposit and share large quantities of information without bogging down e-mail servers and inboxes.)

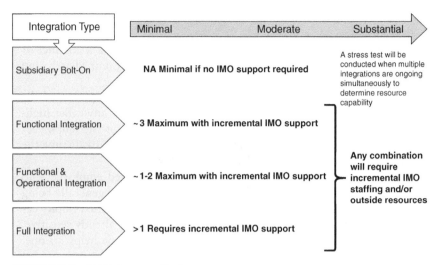

EXHIBIT 7.1 IMO Support Options

Exhibits 7.2 and 7.3 show samples of typical IMOs for an average functional and operational integration and how they would look. This type of sample might serve as the official view for the IMO that you share with stakeholders in the organization.

The key reporting elements can include the following:

- The IMO may report to C-suite (typically, the chief operating officer, but this can vary).
- The IMO may include a division sponsor if one part of the company is heavily involved in the integration (but this is not mandatory).
- An IMO team leader, who may be the executive in charge of the IMO (for whom a typical title is vice president IMO).
- An IMO team support, which may include a mix of dedicated staffers, consulting resources, and administrative support staff.
- Functional integration team leaders. The functions included on your chart may vary, based on the companies' industries and the overall integration type, but it is most common to always have HR, legal, IT, sales, finance and accounting, and operations team leaders. The most important point here is to identify which functions will serve a primary role in the integration activities and to make sure they are represented.

Exhibit 7.4 shows an at-a-glance breakdown of primary roles and responsibilities of the IMO organizational layers. It is critical that these

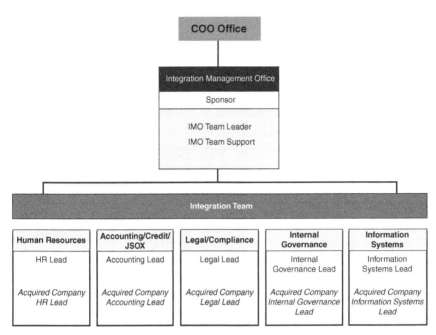

EXHIBIT 7.2   IMO Organizational Model Example

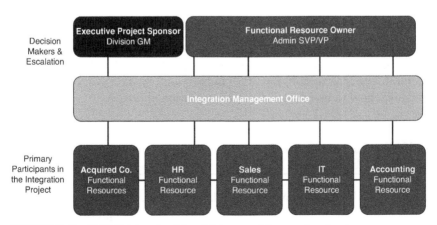

EXHIBIT 7.3   IMO Bridges Decision Makers and Integration Leads

	Integration Process	Accountable For
Project Sponsor	•Charter establishment •Weekly reviews	•Establishing and managing project scope •Issue resolution
Acquired Company Management	•Depends on integration strategy and future role within company, e.g., ranges from no role to that equivalent to functional resource owner	•Committing resources to integration projects
Integration Management Office	•All	•Operating project, communication, and synergy management processes
Functional Resource Owner	• Issue resolution within the function	•Committing resources to integration projects •Communicating resource constraints to IMO
Functional Resource	•Charter review and approval •Weekly reviews •Cross-functional collaboration •Issue identification, escalation, and resolution	•Defining and executing integration projects •Providing periodic status updates

EXHIBIT 7.4   IMO Roles and Responsibilities

activities are established and agreed on in advance and then documented, so they can be shared with the team members before the bulk of integration activity commences.

Adapting the Structure to Fit Your Integration Type

Once you've identified the integration type, you can tweak your organizational structure to align with your integration needs. Exhibit 7.5 shows some structural reporting options based on integration type that you can review to evaluate how to best structure your integration approach.

DETERMINING FUNCTIONAL RESOURCE COMMITMENTS

Functional leads are essential to a smooth integration, and making sure they understand their roles and responsibilities is critical. Integrations can get bogged down unnecessarily because of breakdowns in even one lead's or department's functioning.

	New Subsidiary Acquisition "Functional"	Integrate Subsidiary Elements "Operational"	Absorb Acquired Subsidiary within Existing Subsidiary "Takeover"/"Bolt-On"
Example	Integration A	Integration B	Integration C
Focus Areas	Accounting Corporate Governance HR IT/JSOX	All elements of functional and operational elements required to achieve strategic positioning or synergy goals	All elements of the target business
Integration Project Sponsor	Division sponsor	Division sponsor and subsidiary lead	Division sponsor and subsidiary lead
IMO Reports to	Division sponsor	Subsidiary lead and division sponsor	Division sponsor and subsidiary lead

EXHIBIT 7.5   IMO Structural Reporting Options

In setting up your IMO plan, you also need to establish clear roles for a functional resource owner (e.g., the vice president of finance, whom your integration finance lead reports to) so that he or she knows what to expect as well. To this end, here is a summary of key roles for the manager of a functional resource and for an integration team member.

The manager of a functional resource does the following:

- Allocates and supports the assigned functional resource.
- Manages escalation with functional management.
- Maintains consistency of processes.

An integration team member, in contrast, does the following:

- Is the single point of contact for the IMO as well as its peer functions and the acquired company.
- Has his or her own definition and execution of the functional work plan within the organization.
- Trains or coaches acquired company peers on key business processes.
- Escalates integration-related issues within the function.

<u>**Functional Lead Objectives**</u>
• The integration functional lead is a focal point for accomplishing all functional work, including the development of integration work plans, issue management, and documentation and integration closing activities.

<u>**Functional Lead Core Responsibilities**</u>
• Serve as a member of the integration management office (IMO) for division integrations for a period of 60–90 days on average (time commitment will vary by integration)
• Develop, track, and report functional work-plan progress and issues to the IMO
• Ensure completion and adherence to the scope identified in the integration project charter
• Plan and coordinate overall activities for each specific function
• Participate in IMO integration planning process, and use IMO tools for tracking and communicating information regarding integration activities
• Ensure appropriate links to other functional leads or executives to minimize overlap and to foster efficient coordination among functions

<u>**Recommended Selection Criteria**</u>
• Senior manager level
• Technical expertise/credibility in functional area
• Strong leadership competence
• Conceptual and analytical abilities
• Comfort with ambiguity
• Sense of urgency, action orientation
• Strong people and relationship skills
• Strong planning skills
• Facilitation/cross-functional collaboration and group-process skills
• Strong coaching skills to support acquired company resources through change

EXHIBIT 7.6   Functional Lead Formal Job Description

- Ensures consistency between function status reporting and integration reporting.
- Supports project, synergy, and communication planning and execution as well as individuals from integration project to integration project.

Sometimes it is helpful to create a formal job description for a functional resource lead. Exhibit 7.6 shows a sample of what that might look like in a typical integration.

DEDICATED VERSUS MATRIXED RESOURCES

Dedicated resources are personnel who are solely devoted to integration activity. This means that the integration is their day job, so to speak. Matrixed resources are personnel who have been loaned to the IMO but who still report to their home functions and have other responsibilities.

You might ask which is best during your integration planning. The honest answer is "It depends." If an integration is likely to last more than 120 days and/or is going to be followed by another acquisition and

	Description	Advantages	Disadvantages
Dedicated IMO & Staff	Functional subject matter experts (SMEs) report to IMO	• Integration work is prioritized • Works best in an acquirer/center-of-excellence model	• Function views the functional SME as an external resource, making escalation more difficult • Functional SME career path is typically within the function
Matrixed Resources	• Functional SMEs report to functional resource owners • SMEs support integration projects when required	• Efficient use of functional SMEs • Works best when specific individuals are used consistently from integration to integration	• More stakeholders increases coordination complexity for IMO • Integration work may be treated as a low priority • Requires strong project sponsor commitment to overcome low IMO authority

EXHIBIT 7.7   IMO Staffing Model Options: Advantages and Disadvantages

integration (which happens frequently), and it includes both functional and operational integration activities, then the best option is to secure some dedicated resources. Everything else (or, at least, functional integration) can probably be handled with matrixed resources.

As a general rule, it's better to secure 100 percent of the functional resources time for integration work at the beginning and then relax that restriction once the integration gets under way. This way you have everyone's undivided attention and focus for that critical 30- to 60-day period after the integration officially starts.

If you start off with functional leads being only 50 percent dedicated, for example, they will inevitably be consumed with their day jobs, and their integration work will slip.

Every integration is different, but Exhibit 7.7 shows the advantages and disadvantages of each approach just discussed.

Carefully assessing your staffing needs during due diligence to determine the IMO staffing model that best fits your needs is essential. No one wants to change the IMO structure *during* the integration; changing structures midway is highly undesirable. Get the staffing model agreed on and established up front to help your integration run more smoothly.

SETTING UP AN INTEGRATION PROJECT CHARTER

Integration project charters are recommended for companies that are not experienced acquirers and are thus lacking in integration experience. A charter is a simple document designed to clearly outline the who, what, and how elements of an integration and to gain commitments from resource owners in advance.

Having a charter forces you to have tough discussions before integration activities heat up, so you can resolve difficult conversations in advance. The charter document below is simple and can be modified to reflect the needs of your specific integration. This can include customizations for the following:

- Integration strategy, including functional and operational areas.
- Integration project scope, which is defined as the establishment of some general expectations about the role of the IMO and from where in the organization it will be administered. Bullet points in a scoping document could include the following examples:
  - How integration support will be managed by the chief operations officer (COO).
  - How the integration-support time frame will begin 30 days before the closing and average 90 to 120 days after the closing for the majority of work streams.
  - That the integration playbook (assuming the company has one) will be utilized as the foundation for integration planning.
  - That some integrations may require ad hoc support or playbook augmentation to support unique integration scenarios and planning needs and that the scope will be adjusted to reflect those changes once more information is known.
- Project constraints like earn-out timing and resource availability.

Checklist for Creating an Integration Project Charter

1. Project title and description, including details on the integration of Company ABC into Company XYZ (referred to as Project A in this list).
2. Integration Project A purpose, including information on the business needs, project justifications, and alignments with strategic plan
3. Integration Project A scope, including planning and management of the short-term initiatives required to integrate the merged or acquired entity. The scope can be changed through approval of the project sponsor and the IMO. (It is recommended that this line be included to prevent the pile-on of operational projects that individual stakeholders may like to add to the scope.)
4. Company XYZ participants for Project A.
5. IMO participants for Project A.

6. IMO responsibility and authority guidelines, including an outline of primary responsibilities of the IMO relative to the project. For example:
   - Is the IMO responsible for coordinating a master integration schedule and delivery dates for functional plans for Project A?
   - What is the IMO's centralized decision-making authority for Project A?
7. Integration Project A schedule, including pre-closing to first 100 days and keeping track of transitioning outstanding items to a thinner end-state management process.
8. Integration resources. For example:
   - IMO and project manager roles and stakeholder communication.
   - Integration team functions and organizational charts, including resource commitments and participation levels.
9. Known stakeholder requirements, including project sponsors, functional managers and employees at both the acquired and acquiring companies, integration team members and their managers, as well as customers, investors, and stakeholders in the community.
10. Functional resources requirements and core responsibilities, including the following:
    - Serving as a member of the IMO for division integrations for 60 to 90 days, on average (time commitment will vary by integration).
    - Developing track and reporting functional work-plan progress and issues to the IMO.
    - Ensuring completion and adherence to the scope identified in the integration project charter.
    - Planning and coordinating overall activities for their specific function.
    - Participating in the IMO integration planning process and using IMO tools for tracking and communicating information regarding integration activities.
    - Ensuring appropriate links to other functional leaders or executives to minimize overlap and to foster efficient coordination among functions.
11. Project deliverables, including the integration, communication, and synergy plans; weekly status and lessons-learned reports; and the end-state tracking log.
12. Organizational, environmental, and internal and external assumptions and constraints—including deal terms that may affect schedule, scope, or cost—and resource limitations (e.g., ability, quantity) that need to be factored into the plan.
13. Integration budget management considerations.

The integration project charter should then be reviewed and signed by the project sponsor, IMO participants, and functional resource owners.

While they are reviewing the charter document, the functional resource owners should consider the following questions:

- What resources are required from the business function?
- What are they accountable for?
- When will their project commitments be complete?

Once the charter is reviewed and signed, you can treat the process like a contract between you (the integration manager) and others in the structure whose support is required for executing the integration.

SETTING UP AN INTEGRATION GOVERNANCE STRUCTURE

Governance can be a sensitive topic during an integration (or at any time, for that matter) because often the executive ranks and reporting structures are partly undefined. Exhibit 7.8 shows a sample governance structure for an integration project.

A formalized governance structure is essential to have established while you are creating your charter documents and deciding on structure and

Initial Plan Type or Changes to Plan	Project Sponsor (Executive & Support)	Integration Management Office	Newco Functional Resource Owner	Newco Functional Resource	Acquired Company Resources
Integration Project Charter	A/P	P	C	C	
Integration Project Plan Baseline	A/P	P (Program Level)	C	P (Project Level)	C
Integration Project Plan Baseline Changes	A/P	P	C	P	C
Communication Plan	A/P	P	C	P	C
Synergy Initiative Baseline	A/P	P (Program Level)	C	P (Synergy Initiative Level)	C
Synergy Initiative Baseline Changes	A/P	P	C	P	C
Issue Resolution	A/P	P	P	P	C

EXHIBIT 7.8 Governance Decision Authorities (P = Plan, A = Approve, C = Consult)

reporting for your integration. This allows you to make the best decisions for your integration based on many of the factors outlined in this chapter. It is better to have it and not need it than to need it and end up scrambling to create it after the fact.

CHAPTER CHECKLIST

Here is a list of things to make sure you address as you establish your IMO:

☐ Verify your integration type.
☐ Establish your IMO structure and reporting guidelines.
☐ Establish formalized IMO roles and responsibilities.
☐ Create job descriptions for functional resource commitments.
☐ Establish your integration charter.
☐ Make sure you have a governance structure for your IMO.

SUMMARY

In this chapter we learned some optimal methods and steps for setting up an IMO.

The next chapter reviews the steps, tools, and processes to use in the execution stage of your integration.

CHAPTER 8

Executing Your Integration Plan

I n this chapter, you will learn the following:

- Creating functional integration work streams.
- Prioritizing integration work.
- Understanding work-stream timing and cross-functional dependencies.
- Seeing which areas require extra focus in some functional work-plan examples.

Prior to beginning the execution of your integration plan, make sure you have the pre-planning activities in the previous chapters wrapped up, especially in terms of the following:

- Collecting and reviewing data documentation of both the acquiring and acquired companies.
- Creating and approving the integration project charter for your integration plan, including the IMO setup.
- Formulating the integration team's organizational structure as well as its members' roles and responsibilities.

After you have gone through the steps in creating and coordinating your integration plan up to this point, next it's important to develop your initial integration plans with your functional resource contacts. At the highest level, concentrate your efforts in three key areas:

1. *Your initial integration project plans.* This includes defining the key elements, such as legacy functional work plans and drafts of integration work plans for key functions (e.g., the integration work plan for the HR team).
2. *Your communication plan.* It is important to clarify two key integration terms before you delve into execution. Day one most often means the

day a deal officially closes and is announced to the press (sometimes it is referred to as day 0). There is also what's known as employee day one. It is when employees are notified of the acquisition and briefed on the next steps and/or introduced to their new management team. For both of these epic events, communication is critical from the very start in order to manage the integration well.

3. *Your synergy initiative plan.* Formulating a solid approach to synergy planning and realization of the integration is critical to preserving deal value and achieving the expected synergies within the specified time frames needed. (There are examples of documents and tools to support synergy work streams later in this book to help you make this process easier.)

FUNCTIONAL WORK-PLAN ELEMENTS

A functional work plan is a compilation of projects and initiatives that are integration related, most of which will start and end within the integration time frame. Exhibit 8.1 is a high-level snapshot of the most basic functional work-plan elements to help get you started with executing your integration plan.

The format can vary. Use templates or project management tools that your organization is already familiar with to help speed up adoption. Functional work plans are essential to leading your IMO and functional leader

	Inputs	Outputs
(1) Initial Integration Project Plan	• Integration project charter (includes high-level strategy) • Due diligence data • Legacy functional work plans	• Draft functional work plans • Initial draft of issue log
(2) Initial Communication Plan	• Stakeholder analysis • Legacy communication products	• Initial communication plan • Day 0 communications • Focus on first 30 days
(3) Initial Synergy Initiative Plan	• Anticipated deal benefit target opportunities *(typically available with executive approval package for deal)*	• Initial synergy benefit plan • Opportunities requiring further business case analysis and planning

EXHIBIT 8.1 Essential Work-Plan Elements

teams to getting your plan done well and on time. They include all of the action items associated with a specific function, like those in HR, IT, and sales. Important items to include in your plan are the following:

- A description of the initiative.
- Status colors, such as using green, yellow, and red to note where a particular part of a project is in terms of the process.
- A list of the accountable owners, showing who is responsible for completing particular parts of the projects within each business function.
- A list of integration leaders or contacts. Depending on the scope of a particular part of an organization's involvement, this list may assign an individual to manage and be responsible for the status of a particular part of the project portfolio within that function
- A targeted completion date.
- Dependencies and other team members involved in working on particular parts of the integration plan.
- Any notes, like those maintained on a weekly basis to provide a view of current status and issues and to facilitate cross-functional collaborations.
- Some integration plans may require detail on costs as well (sometimes called costs to achieve). These are the costs associated specifically with an integration work stream (e.g., closing a facility).

It is strongly advised that you consider a project management tool to organize all of these functional work-plan elements. Software applications like Daptiv and Inchieve have customized fields for integration activities but also have tons of flexibility for layering in project management fields and expanding your capabilities, so the tool is essentially configured to match the needs of your integration. Better yet, it gives you many ways to cut and sort different data to help with your executive reporting needs.

If you have integration activities involving more than a few functions (and who doesn't?), check out a software planning tool to make your integration run more smoothly. It will allow you to have a centralized planning tool that everyone can use consistently and easily.

INTEGRATION WORK STREAMS

Probably the most frequently asked question at the beginning of integration planning is "What is an integration work stream?" Many definitions might be obvious at first, but the bulk of work-stream activities requires functional leaders to assess key areas of their departments to determine what should be integrated and how.

At the highest level, integration work streams can include the following:

- The projects or initiatives that might help you to achieve savings and benefits from an integration (e.g., better contracting and labor reduction due to duplication of functions).
- The functions that can be integrated to make managing parts of your plan easier so you have just one policy and process to oversee (e.g., integrating employee discipline, HR, financial assistance policies, and payroll cycles)
- Strategic alignments and value (e.g., branding, marketing, system measurement, and reporting components).
- Any area where two versions of a similar process, policy, or specific way of doing business might cause delays or disruption and limit productivity when integrating Company ABC with Company XYZ.

Exhibit 8.2 shows a snapshot of some high-level prioritization guidance to advise your functional leads as they begin to develop their integration plans.

Prioritization is incredibly important because you may find you have several hundred work streams when integrating Company ABC with Company XYZ. At some point, some executive along the way is going to say,

High
- Projects or Initiatives that will achieve savings and benefits from the integration
- Any areas where maintaining 2 versions of a similar process, policy, or specific way of doing business will cause disruption and slow our evolution to the newco.

Med
- Functions that will have to be integrated to make managing easier and to have just one policy and process (i.e., employee discipline policies, payroll cycles, HR policies, financial assistance policies)
- Any work stream that has strategic alignment and value (i.e., branding, marketing, system measurement, and reporting)

Low
- Essentially any work stream that does not fit into the high or medium categories
- Any work stream longer than 12 months that has no significant HR, service level, or operations disruption impacts

EXHIBIT 8.2   Work-Plan Prioritization

"Show me the top 10 work streams," so having a list and prioritizing it is essential.

In an integration, any cost savings or revenue-enhancement initiatives should be a high priority because synergy realization is always the most critical deliverable of any integration. If integration work streams are included in plans but not marked as high priorities, you should work with your functional leader to get them labeled as such so you can put the appropriate degree of focus on the included initiatives.

FUNCTIONAL WORK-PLAN QUALITY

Exhibit 8.3 includes a snapshot of a typical functional work plan for HR. These are just a few of the many dozens of items that are typically included in a work plan (the HR department, especially, tends to have many more items than other departments), so this is just to give you an idea.

Human Resources				
STATUS: INITIATIVES		OWNER	TARGETED COMPLETION	COMMENTS
C	Finalize Joe M. consultant agreement			Completed
C	Terminate stock option agreements for Keith R.			Completed
C	**New Offer Letters: APA**. Creation of new offer letters for all acquired company employees			Completed
C	**HR Integration Strategy**. Develop HR functional integration strategy (to be reviewed with IMO). This strategy would include functional work plan, key milestones, time line, and responsible person in charge.			Completed

EXHIBIT 8.3 Functional Work-Plan Example

Again, the format in which you list the work-plan items should be dictated by the needs of your particular integration, but it is imperative that each function lead be responsible for submitting a detailed plan prior to employee day one.

Unfortunately, the quality and degree of detail in functional work plans can vary considerably among submissions. Despite a common template designed to mitigate such issues, the quality of the input is largely dictated by the skills and available time of the functional resource who is assigned to the IMO (e.g., the HR person who has been assigned to work on HR integration work streams).

Here is an important tip if you are unsatisfied with the level of detail of a functional work plan: Work directly with the owner to layer in the necessary details and input rather than sending the plan back to the owners for reworking. Remember, most functional resource owners have other responsibilities in addition to dealing with your needs, so a little understanding at the outset goes a long way, especially if your integration will last for several months.

Below are some tips by category to help you ensure that functional work plans have the level of detail required to support your integration. If the functional work plan seems to be lacking detail or is incomplete, you can check it against considerations in these areas.

Project Timing Timing questions to consider can include the following:

- Is the starting date too late?
- Are the durations too long?
- Are the end dates undefined?

If these questions have not been answered, the work plan needs some additional care and tweaking. It is important to fully define your timing parameters, because once you get into reporting on the integration progress, anything that is lagging in the schedule will be marked yellow or red (i.e., delayed) and will become a point of focus for company executives. Since no one wants to be the functional leader with the tardy work streams, it is best to get these clarified early and be conservative and overdeliver, rather than the opposite.

Project Details Functional leaders are often great at loading in the overview of an entire project but lack in providing the many details of the specific initiatives that are important to a successful integration. If there seems to be detail lacking in the integration projects, it is best to pause and get the details prior to locking the plans down. Adding details as you go is somewhat expected, but trying to define entire work streams while you are supposedly executing will lead to incomplete work and poor results.

Cross-Functional Dependencies Functional work streams are often dependent on something else getting accomplished. For example, a newly integrated HR system or policy may require an IT software enhancement or upgrade. When IT has to do something before HR can, it needs to be identified early so that both functions communicate with each other. This way they are in sync.

Isolating cross-functional dependencies can be challenging for a variety of reasons, and integration managers should note that cross-functional issues are typically rooted out and are not always obvious. Here are some reasons that getting clarify on cross-functional issues can be difficult:

- *Incomplete work plans.* If one function has not isolated all of the necessary integration initiatives for its area, then it becomes difficult to identify issues because they simply are not obvious. An example might be an HR initiative that is inherent in a new software implementation; however, the need for the software and the IT implementation required to operationalize it have not been identified as an integration initiative. In this case HR is dependent on IT, but IT has no idea, since the need for new software has not been identified.
- *Staffing needs.* Sometimes initiatives for one function can't be completed without support from another. An example is an organization that needs new sales training, but the personnel who administer the training are not hired yet, or perhaps the training organization is still being defined. In this case, sales can't sell the new products without the training, and thus a product rollout is dependent on the training group being fully functional.
- *Business and strategic guidance.* Sometimes functions can't fully develop their plans because they require strategic and/or operating plan guidance. As discussed in earlier chapters on pre-planning, getting as many of an organization's strategy and business objectives defined and articulated prior to the integration work commencing is critically important. Functions affected the most by this type of scenario are finance and IT, since the allocation and funding of IT resources are often dictated by organizational strategy and operating needs.

Organizational Dependencies Sometimes there are high-level organizational dynamics that need to be clarified before integration work streams can be better defined. The most common types of issues here can include questions about the following:

- *Decision rights.* These include information on which executive or function owns the decision rights for a particular area of the business.
- *Organizational structures.* This can cause delays and problems if the integration leaders do not know whom to work with. Defining the organizational structures of both companies can reduce these issues.
- *Staff reductions.* Usually there are reductions in force (RIF) in integrations, and until the integrations are completed, RIFs can often impede integration progress.
- *Cultural integration.* As briefly mentioned in a prior chapter, solving cultural issues should be made a priority. It is an important work stream because there may be cultural issues at the senior-executive level that need to be mitigated before other integration work streams can progress to your satisfaction.

FUNCTIONS REQUIRING EXTRA ATTENTION

All execution-preparatory functions require some degree of attention, but some will need your extra-careful attention. The way the following areas are handled will affect almost every other work stream, especially if they are off track or poorly managed.

Human Resources

HR work streams and work plans are critically important in order to help create a nearly flawless integration plan between the HR departments of Company ABC and Company XYZ. This should be a huge area of focus for the IMO and functional leads, because poor HR planning can cripple an integration for weeks or months.

The people parts of integrations are the hardest aspects to manage, and if your people are anxious about benefits and policies, for instance, they will be less productive as a result. Your HR leads need to communicate early and often about HR work streams to both their functional leads and the organizations. Ideally, HR functional leads can communicate HR information through the other IMO functional leads for dissemination throughout the organizations.

Here are some examples of high-impact HR work streams that often require some extra attention:

- Policy and process consolidation

This item is first because it typically generates the most questions, and if left undefined it will cause you an inordinate number of headaches. Here are some of the items needed to define the policy and process work stream:

- Overtime policy
- Bereavement policy
- Holiday policy
- Drug and alcohol policy
- New hire screening policy
- Independent contractors policy
- Remote workforce policy
- Employee code of ethics and conduct policies
- Attendance and tardiness policies
- Workplace safety standards and policies
- Relocation policy
- Rehire process policy
- Corrective action and termination policy
- Length of service bridge process
- Workplace harassment policies
- Reward and service recognition policies
- HR broker and consultant consolidation
- Employee discount program consolidation
- Continuing education program consolidation

There are probably two dozen more considerations like these that all need to be consolidated as part of HR policy and process integration. Other HR work streams to pay close attention to include the following:

- Benefits policy consolidation
- Performance evaluation and measurement alignment
- Payroll integration
- Retirement plans consolidation
- Compensation policy integration
- Job description alignment
- Labor relations policies
- Diversity policies

It is very important to make sure your HR integration planning is as comprehensive and complete as possible. HR can be, and often is, the highest-generating center of activity in any integration.

Here's why you can't avoid or delay HR policy and process integration:

- *Cost.* The longer you have to support two versions of every policy and process, the more expensive it will be, because it will require duplicate systems and personnel.
- *Culture.* You can't even begin to mesh cultures until everyone is in the same policy and process structure. If one group gets more paid vacation days than another, the disaffected group will resent it.
- *Collaboration.* It's hard for two groups to work together if they have to accommodate varying methods of performance evaluations, hiring guidelines, and the numerous areas listed above. The longer you have two versions of the same policy and process, the harder it will be to assimilate workforces and accelerate productivity.

Information Technology

IT is important because integration here typically takes the longest and can be the most expensive. The most important thing is to get the IT work streams defined as best as possible so the organization can better understand what systems are going to be integrated and when. Lack of clarity in integrating the IT departments of Company ABC and Company XYZ can be a sore spot for everyone involved in the integration. IT is always one of the more understaffed areas of a company; hence there are scant resources available to focus on integration activities when they arise.

Here are some examples of high-impact IT work streams that often require some extra attention:

- Consolidation of intranet and Internet properties.
- Common e-mail and desktop platforms.
- Integration of billing solutions.
- IT support vendor consolidation.
- Mobile equipment and policy consolidation.
- IT consolidation needs for customer care or call centers.
- System rationalization process (e.g., a process to make decisions on which IT software or hardware to use for specific applications, since each company might have its own version and the combined company only needs one).

Finance

Integrating the finance departments of two companies in a merger or an acquisition is always difficult because integrating accounting systems and financial policies is hard, detailed work. By keeping finance departments on the list of priorities, the IMO leaders can figure out if they are able to provide additional help to their financial integration leaders. These leaders typically need lots of assistance because the systems are so complex.

Here are some examples of high-impact finance work streams that often require some extra attention:

- Accounting integration
- Accounts payable integration
- Reporting guidelines and package consolidation
- Payroll integration (policies, processes, and software)

Here are some additional examples of some functional work streams and initiatives to be mindful of in your integration planning:

- *Corporate governance.* Consolidation of various governing boards, oversight committees, advisory boards, and others.
- *Marketing.* Ad agency and media buying consolidation, external web site and social media consolidation.
- *Facilities.* Office and plant consolidation.
- *Legal and insurance.* Legal service consolidation (e.g., law firm rationalization) and insurance provider consolidation.
- *Operations.* Procurement policies and equipment vendor consolidation.

CHAPTER CHECKLIST

Here are some key areas to focus on as part of the execution phase of your integration:

- ☐ Define what you expect to be included in each functional work stream.
- ☐ Clearly define the timing parameters for integration work streams.
- ☐ Identify cross-functional dependencies.
- ☐ Pay careful attention to HR, finance, and IT work streams.

SUMMARY

In this chapter, we learned how to establish functional integration work streams and what some of the specific areas are to define the work.

Next we will review how to transition your integration to end state and officially close the IMO. All good things come to an end, including integrations.

CHAPTER 9

Planning Your Integration's End State

I n this chapter, you will learn the following:

■ How to define the end state for your integration.
■ The end state process and steps required to officially wrap up your integration.
■ Tips and strategies to make sure you finish well.

Every integration needs to have an end. Planning for your end state is just as important as planning the integration itself. One of the most important activities you can do early to make the end state a fairly simple activity is to clearly scope out at the beginning of the integration what your end state is.

Pre-planning is the ideal time to decide on a recommended time frame for the bulk of integration activities. The recommended time frame for most integration activities is 90 to 120 days.

Of course, some work streams will get done early, and some (like IT systems integrations) may take as long as 12 to 24 months before they are technically finished.

For the purposes of integration planning, the end state can be defined as follows:

■ The point in the integration at which most of the planned integration activities are accomplished.
■ The transition point, when the IMO processes can be ramped down and dedicated IMO personnel scaled back or redeployed.
■ The point at which the remaining open integration work streams and issues can be transitioned to functional teams.

HOW TO KNOW WHEN AN INTEGRATION IS FINISHED

End state is an extremely difficult concept to grasp for most integration managers, since work streams never seem to be fully complete and it is sometimes difficult to get formal documentation that something is actually finished.

One of the methods you can use to get a better grasp of end state is to define it up front. Now, defining end state for every integration project would be almost impossible, so focus on the highest-priority areas for your integration and work with your assigned functional leaders to map out the following for a particular project by a specified date:

- What is the desired experience for the employees and other internal stakeholders for this integration project? For example, all employees will have a commonly formatted e-mail address (firstname.lastname @newco.com), all employees will have access to the common intranet site, and all legacy intranet sites will be "sunseted" (essentially decommissioned or closed).
- What is the desired end state for our customers? For example, all customers will have access to the full array of newco products and services, and pricing will be uniform throughout our distribution footprint.
- What is the desired end state for the community? For example, our legacy community outreach and charitable programs will be consolidated, and we will speak to the communities we operate it in the unified voice of our new company.
- What is the desired end state for marketing? For example, we will market under our newco brand name and logo in all the markets we serve.

For all of the above scenarios (which are pretty basic), the articulation of a defined end state helps integration project leaders to make sure the right things get done within a specified time frame.

It is absolutely necessary to define integration projects with some articulation of the end state. If you don't, you may see a lot of activity but little being done to force real change and a different way of doing business. As an integration leader, it is *your* responsibility to force this level of clarity out of the most critical integration work streams.

THE TYPICAL PROCESS: ROLES, RESPONSIBILITIES, TRACKING, AND FINISHING WELL

At the conclusion of the IMO oversight of the integration management process, outstanding work-plan elements should be collected, organized by

	Due Diligence	Integration		End State Monitoring
Goal	Planning & Execution		Feedback & Optimization	
When	Pre-Close	First 30 Days	30 – 100 Days	> 100 Days
Activities	• NA	• NA	• Begin collection of long-term functional work-plan elements	• Document open functional work-plan elements, deliverables, timing, accountability, etc. • Begin end state tracking process • Facilitate lessons-learned process and coordinate employee/stakeholder survey administration

EXHIBIT 9.1   End State High-level Process/Activities

function, and formally transferred to that function. This process typically occurs at day 100 of most integrations, but it can occur earlier or later, at the discretion of the IMO.

The IMO should facilitate a weekly end state call with all functions for 30 days following day 100. At day 130, any remaining end state issues are formally documented, and IMO involvement concludes. This transition allows for adequate information transfer, as some of the personnel taking on the functional work streams may be new to the integration, the function, the company, or all of the above

Exhibit 9.1 shows how the end state factors into a typical integration time frame.

It is extremely important to clearly define the end state process. This includes clearly documenting and properly transitioning as follows:

- Documenting can typically be done using Excel or some other project management tool, and each end state initiative should have details about remaining open issues, owners, and planned date of completion.
- Transitioning should be done through a formal process of calls or meetings in which the open initiative is officially handed off. At this point, the initiative becomes just another action item for a particular function and ceases being an integration work stream or project.

The risk of poorly executed end state planning is that integration issues get orphaned and become problems for someone else down the road. This is a critical juncture, since end state initiatives can sometimes be major items, not just trivial action items with no urgency. One example is plant or facilities closing. These typically take longer to complete and will outrun an IMO, so they have to be transitioned as end state action items.

It takes longer to close facilities for a variety of reasons, including the time required to exit a lease, clean up a site (especially if it was a manufacturing facility), or transition production. This means that someone has to make sure the site closes by the specified time frame, because there is a cost savings target associated with that closure. Therefore, pay attention to all end state work streams and make sure they are handed off so the new owner has the following:

- Documentation of deadlines and deliverables associated with the remaining open items.
- Access to all documentation on the project.
- A list of all contacts and stakeholders involved in the project.
- A full understanding of what has to be done, by when and by whom. Most important, make sure the new owner has an understanding of the negative implications of the project getting delayed.

If end state handoffs are not processed properly, guess who typically gets the blame? The IMO! So don't let poor end state planning ruin an otherwise well-executed integration.

Exhibit 9.2 shows a typical breakdown of end state process high-level roles and responsibilities.

	Role	Accountable For
Integration Management Office	Facilities weekly calls and consolidates reporting	Collecting, monitoring progress, expediting completion
Functional Resource Owner	Provides functional resource for end state tracking	Ensuring functional resource remains engaged thru end state issue completion
Functional Resource *(Functional Lead)*	Monitoring and reporting on end state issue progress and participating in weekly calls	End state issue resolution
Acquired Company Functional Resource	May be involved in end state issue resolution	Assisting functional owner with end state issue resolution

EXHIBIT 9.2   End State Roles and Responsibilities

Integration A: End State Work Plan

Status	Milestone / Deliverable	Owner	Due Date	Comments
	Overall Status			
	Accounting			
On Target				
On Target				
On Target				
	Human Resources			
On Target				
On Target				
On Target				
On Target				
	Finance			
On Target				
On Target				
On Target				
On Target				
	Information Systems			
On Target				
On Target				
On Target				
On Target				
	Legal/Compliance			
On Target				
On Target				
On Target				
On Target				
	Operations			
On Target				
On Target				
	Marketing			
On Target				
	TBD			
On Target				
On Target				

EXHIBIT 9.3   End State Work-Plan Example

At day 130 (or the specific date designated by the IMO, if other than 130), IMO involvement should conclude, and any remaining issues are then documented, handed off, and the responsibility of the new company's functional owners.

A formal handoff meeting is highly recommended, with each functional leader present to ensure that end state tracking issues are clearly defined. This also gives the functional owner a chance to ask any clarifying questions before the IMO exits the process.

Exhibit 9.3 is a sample end state tracking log for collecting and managing remaining end state issues.

When you are finishing up an integration process, ensure that all outstanding integration work-plan elements have clear ownership, clear accountability for resolution, and an expected time frame for completion before you hand off the project to the new company's functional owners.

End state can be a confusing concept and process, because integration work is complex and sometimes feels like it's never officially finished. In this regard, end state planning is important because it signals that the integration phase of the acquisition or merger is officially over and that a transition to normalized operations is required.

Transferring any remaining work activity to the functional owners is important—it provides a home for the remaining work so it becomes a normal business activity for that function. The key is to hand off any remaining work so it's easy to complete and finish.

CHAPTER CHECKLIST

Overall, here are a few tips for executing a successful end state handoff:

- ☐ Make sure each initiative is handed off with all previous activity (e.g., decks, spreadsheets), so the new organization has all of the historical artifacts it needs.
- ☐ If necessary, articulate end state scenarios for high-priority projects.
- ☐ Meet with the senior leadership of any functions receiving end state issues, to review, discuss, and recommend actions and to confirm the official handoff.
- ☐ Provide the functional personnel with any contact information for the integration team in case there are questions down the road that need clarification.

SUMMARY

In this chapter, we reviewed how to execute the end state phase of an integration and how to transition an integration to a successful close.

In the next few chapters, we delve deeper into these key integration areas: communication planning, cultural integration, talent assessment, and synergy program management.

CHAPTER 10

Effective Communication Planning

In this chapter, you will learn the following:

■ Objectives and guiding principles for effective integration communication.
■ How to create a communication matrix for your integration.
■ Roles and responsibilities for communication planning within the integration management office.

Communication planning is one of the most written-about subjects in integration-related books and articles because it's one of the most important activities of integration. Often it is the subject that IMO leaders struggle with the most. This is mainly due to the following:

■ Information itself is closely guarded or unavailable, so meaningful content becomes hard to get in the first place.
■ Senior executives do not always buy into sound or frequent communication planning, and they disregard pleas for meaningful content and news.
■ Communication is always great when the deal closes and on employee day one, but it typically will quickly fade after that.

Because having a proper communication plan is key, this chapter addresses the steps you can take to ensure that the communication portion of your plan is as robust as the rest of your integration plan.

COMMUNICATION PLANNING OBJECTIVES

The following objectives can offer you the tools you need to create a solid foundation for your communication plan:

■ Define what the employees from both organizations can expect during the integration process.

- Ensure that the employees understand the integration goals and processes.
- Provide the employees with an understanding of the new company's organizational structure and operational goals.
- Reinforce the acquiring company's executives' high level of commitment to the integration.
- Ensure that the IMO is engaged in all aspects of the integration process with ongoing visits to acquired-company locations.
- Ensure that various feedback mechanisms are in place to collect and address issues as they arise.
- Put safeguards in place to improve the speed of acceptance for change, as documented in the employee survey results (more on this in Chapter 15).

GUIDING PRINCIPLES FOR AN EFFECTIVE COMMUNICATION PLAN

Overall, there are a number of guiding principles for making an effective communication plan. The following areas of focus are essential:

- *Frequency, frequency, frequency.* Plan your communications so that you have ample opportunities to dispense information at regular intervals. Err on the side of overcommunicating, if anything.
- *Honesty.* Open and honest communication goes a long way toward calming anxiety and keeping people focused during an integration. Avoid harboring information that could be shared or limiting the distribution of information to a select few within a company.
- *Specificity of messaging.* Communications and messages should be tailored to the audience they are intended for. Don't blast communications that might be irrelevant to portions of your audience.
- *Attention to feedback.* Always have a channel to collect feedback and make sure to properly address the feedback in subsequent communications.
- *Personalized messages.* Do this wherever and whenever possible, as stakeholders will appreciate communication more when it addresses issues and topics of particular relevance to them.
- *Authoritative communications.* Make sure that communications come from recognized leaders in the company, especially those who are an established presence among the acquired employees. In addition, make sure to always craft the messages to address employee perspectives on what is happening, why it is happening, and what it means for them.

Despite having what seems like a recipe for disaster, you can prevail and succeed at creating a robust communication plan in advance of employee day one by remembering that communication is one of the most important components of your integration plan. Communication lapses are the issues that acquired employees complain about most when asked to provide post-integration feedback. Effective communication is a constant struggle, but it is worth it, so get your senior stakeholders to provide the most informative and specific input needed to build a solid communication plan.

ESTABLISHING A COMMUNICATION MATRIX

Exhibit 10.1 shows a simple communication planning matrix, which should always include the following inputs:

- *Audience.* Who are the stakeholder groups requiring communication? This information should include all of the groups you can think of, even if some of those groups may require a simple, onetime notification.
- *Objectives.* What behaviors or outcomes are required by the functional leaders and resource owners? For example, with customers, a key objective during an integration is always to maintain a high rate of retention.

Audience	Objectives (Why)	Key Messages	Vehicles (How)	Timing/Frequency	Ownership (From Whom)	Draft Responsibility
Employees						
Customers						
Suppliers						
Shareholders/ Investors						
Community						
Other						

EXHIBIT 10.1   Communication Matrix Example

- *Key messages.* What are the facts that the employees, as well as anyone the integrating companies interact with, need to know?
- *Message vehicles.* How are messages sent to the audience you are trying to reach? Note that sometimes you may need to create a new vehicle where one does not yet exist. For instance, you could create an integration e-letter (a newsletter that can be distributed by e-mail) and title it *Newco News.*
- *Timing and frequency.* When communicating with your audience, make sure to include specific dates and outline how often thereafter you will communicate to them. Whenever possible, overcommunicate and specify dates.
- *Ownership.* Who is making the authoritative communication? Is it the CEO, the vice president of IT, or someone else? Decide and then have that leader personalize the message as much as possible.
- *Draft responsibility.* Who creates the communications drafts? The IMO often drafts communication salvos to speed up the process, but note that communications should come from specific people and not the IMO, as a rule.

Communication after Day One

Making a communications plan for the first 45 to 60 days of an integration and planning on the messaging beforehand so you can be developing it earlier versus doing so on the fly is strongly recommended. You can always modify a communication plan based on specific communication needs that arise during the integration, but having a plan laid out in advance is highly advised.

Exhibit 10.2 shows a sample communication plan from day 1 through day 60 (i.e., 60 days past day 1 of an integration).

Don't Just Wing It: Preparing for Employee Day One

It is amazing how some executives think that addressing the employees of an acquired company is like any other meeting. However, it's not, and executives who don't prepare well are laying the groundwork for a bumpy integration by not making communication a priority from the start.

Acquired employees are nervous. They are suspicious and anxious. When this happens, you can guess what they are distracted from most: the very day-to-day operations you are responsible for managing when you are acquiring them!

A smooth employee day one is possible if you do the following:

- Have the right people present. Don't send a middle manager to address everyone; make sure the leaders for key functions are present and, if

Pre-Close	Day 0	Employee Day 1	Employee Day 1+15	Employee Day 1+30	Employee Day 1+60
• Review draft communication plan with acquired company management	• Investor communication triggered	• Employee welcome rally	• Functional leaders communicate regularly regarding Integration progress	• Executive visits; key employee and customer locations	• Compensation and job title changes communicated to all retained employees
• Identify executive, employee, and investor communication channels within acquired company	• CEO employee welcome letter including interim leadership assignments	• Functional messaging aligning acquisition goals to function's mission	• Training team communicates required (regulatory, ethics) training schedule	• Targeted communication; short-term sales incentives	• Integration-specific communication diminishes as employees receive updates via functional management and company leadership
• Brief acquiring company management on communication approach, timing, content	• Functional specific communication and welcome	• HR/Benefits enrollment communication	• Message short-term HR, Finance, and other back-office process/system changes	• Reinforce key actions in weekly employee announcements	
• Coordinate site visit schedule	• Detailed interim management structure announcements	• IT access communication (intranet, e-mail, etc.)		• Target state organization and leadership selection announcements	
	• HR FAQs	• Implement integration progress reporting for employees		• Sales commissions and compensation transition plan communicated	
	• Strategic partner communication	• Establish employee feedback channels			
	• Financial controls and signature authority				

EXHIBIT 10.2 Sample Communication Plan Schedule and Elements

Timing	Actions
Day 1 – April 13 9:45 am	☐ David and Dan to call meeting for senior management at 10:00 am ☐ David to send an e-mail asking all employees to gather for an 11:00 am townhall meeting. Satellite employees are asked to attend via teleconference (no details about the purpose of the meeting are given in the e-mail)
Day 1 10:00 am	☐ David to announce the good news about the acquisition. Explain the timing was right and NEWCO was a good fit ☐ Harry to provide overview of NEWCO: company history and commitment to customers, employees, shareholders, and the community, and why we are excited about our future together, then introduce Brenda/Mike ☐ Brenda/Mike to state how pleased s/he is to have everyone on the NEWCO team, and show NEWCO identity DVD (8 minutes) ☐ Dustin to pass out NEWCO Overview materials for senior managers (annual report, IOP, brochure, org chart). Additional items to be passed out for staff distribution ☐ Open to questions and answers ☐ David to explain that a townhall meeting will be held at 11:00 am to formally announce the good news to the rest of the employees
Day 1 10:00 am	☐ Michelle to open the bridge for dial-in participants (for satellite office participation)
Day 1 – Townhall 11:00 am	☐ David to explain reason for sale and what it will mean to the employees; then introduce Harry ☐ Harry to provide an overview of NEWCO and why he is excited about the future partnership between Aquired Company A and NEWCO and to introduce Brenda/Mike ☐ Brenda/Mike to state how pleased s/he is to have everyone on the NEWCO team ☐ Michelle to explain the HR impacts of the transaction ☐ Michelle to provide take-home materials (announcement, FAQs, org chart, welcome letter from CEO, NEWCO fact sheet, brochure) ☐ David to inform sales team to get in touch with customers/vendors the next day and to keep the information confidential for the time being. Will give sales team language to use if the news leaks and a customer calls before it is made public. David and Michelle will provide e-mail templates and FAQs for announcement purposes
Day 1 12 noon	☐ Lunch with Aquired Company A employees (pizza delivery, opportunity for NEWCO/Aquired Company A interaction)
Day 1 2:00 pm	☐ Kevin to drive to other location to make the announcement regarding the deal – will provide sales team with language to use if the news leaks and a customer calls before the news is made public ☐ David and Kevin to make calls to select vendors regarding the news

EXHIBIT 10.3   Employee Day 1 Meeting Agenda Example

possible, set up a webcast to have your CEO address the employees in real time.

- Script the entire first day (see Exhibit 10.3 for an example).
- Have a plan for continued follow-up ready and in place so you don't create a "one and done" communication event (in which the employees are treated to a big day one event that soon fades and finds them clamoring for more information).
- Collect questions and create a rolling FAQ log, a list of frequently asked questions with answers that can be updated each week as new questions

are asked. This way you have a resource you can send to people who need answers, or you can direct them to a shared site where the FAQ documents can always be found.

The Risk of Poor Communications

Incomplete and/or insufficient communication is one of the most common complaints you hear during an integration. Poor communication can create resentment and confusion among the very people you are trying to retain and motivate to keep business processes going successfully, and it can lead to other unexpected results, including the following:

- *Culture war.* Culture clashes are to be expected, but they can be exacerbated by poor communication planning.
- *Customer defections.* Customers of the acquired company are already wondering what is going to change, so do not give them an excuse to defect by simply failing to communicate with them. Remind them how valuable they are to their new company.
- *Rogue planning efforts.* Employees kept in the dark will start doing their own "integration activities," and many of them can be detrimental to business or overall processes.
- *Stalled productivity.* Employees who lack information, especially about their own situations, can freeze at the wheel and stall a company's productivity.
- *Unexpected costs.* Poor communication can result in acquired employees making financial decisions that result in unnecessary costs being incurred.
- *Poor morale.* This can be a result of a combination of any or all of the above. There are many negative outcomes to poor communication, but the good news is that most of them are preventable.

A PROPER COMMUNICATION PROCESS

Exhibit 10.4 shows effective communication management plan (CMP) processes and timing.

The IMO's role in planning good communication processes can include the following:

- Ensuring that the CMP guiding principles and objectives are in force and that complete and consistent messages are delivered.
- Collaborating with functions on the day 0 content preparation schedule (the IMO may ghostwrite communications as needed).

CMP High-Level Process/Activities			
	Due Diligence	**Integration**	**End State Monitoring**
Goal	Planning & Execution		Feedback & Optimization
When	Pre-Close	First 30 Days	30–100 Days	> 100 Days
Activities	• Identify all stakeholder groups • Agree on and prioritize key messages • Draft all day 0-30 communications • Finalize e-mail distribution lists and other message delivery channels • Create feedback mechanism • Create e-mail templates • Finalize day 0-30 activities and logistics • Finalize communication schedule • Use SharePoint to store communication artifacts • Finalize approval process for ongoing communication needs (e.g., what does or does not have to go thru Legal or HR each time)	• Execute first 30 days communication plan • Monitor and address feedback • Update FAQs • Draft new communications as needed	• CMP project status management • Update FAQs • Draft new communications as needed	• Survey stakeholders • Publish lessons learned • Incorporate changes into integration process • Create repository of all communications used during integration

EXHIBIT 10.4   CMP High-level Process/Activities

- Collaborating with HR and the project sponsor to finalize day 0 content and materials
- Doing a day 0 and employee day 1 communication readiness review (e.g., content ready, message order, delivery vehicle, messengers or proxies, confirmations).
- Receiving status updates through the IMO weekly process when communication has taken place in each function and by executives.
- Updating the executive team.
- Coordinating tactical responses to any urgent questions that may come out of meetings and feedback channels.

Roles, Responsibilities, and Target Audiences

Exhibit 10.5 shows a high-level overview of typical IMO and functional leader roles and responsibilities during CMP.

Note how critical the functional areas are in communication planning. They are generators of content and control the distribution channel. For example, the bulk of integration FAQs are typically centered on HR policies and processes, which are created by the HR function and often distributed via employee-targeted communication channels. In this case, HR is the

	Role	Accountable For
Integration Management Office	Compiles master CMP schedule	Collecting, monitoring progress, expediting completion
Functional Resource Owner	Provides key messages	Ensuring functional resource executes CMP deliverables
Functional Resource *(Functional Lead)*	Drafts and approves communications	Delivery of all stakeholder communications
Acquired Company Functional Resource	May help with collecting and aggregating employee and customer/supplier feedback	TBD (depends on functional resource)

EXHIBIT 10.5   Communication Planning Roles and Responsibilities

creator and distributor of the content, so obviously that department needs to be highly engaged in the CMP.

Exhibit 10.6 shows a matrix of communication audiences for the most typical scenarios that occur during an integration. CMP must address communication needs for all audiences and include guidance on key messages, timing, delivery methods, feedback processes, and IMO tasks.

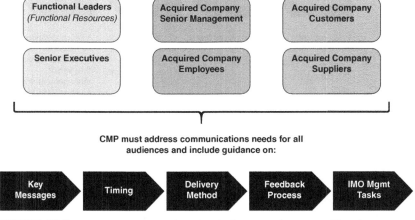

EXHIBIT 10.6   Communication Planning Audience and Content Planning

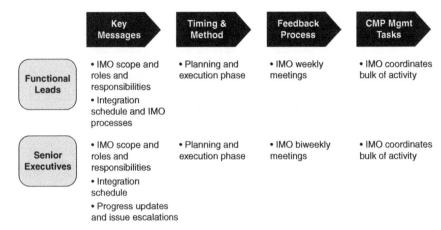

EXHIBIT 10.7   Communication Planning Audience and Content Planning

Note in this example that we have different audiences for communication planning. One version of a message does not fit all. It is critical to craft the right message for the right audience and deliver it at the right time.

Messages by Audience

An important area to consider as you finalize your communication planning is to organize your communications by audience. Exhibit 10.7 shows a grid

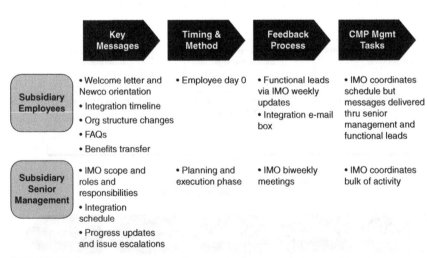

EXHIBIT 10.8   Communication Planning Audience and Content Planning

Key Messages	Timing & Method	Feedback Process	CMP Mgmt Tasks
Subsidiary Customers • Ownership change announcement • Any contact changes	• Day 0	• Collect issues thru subsidiary as needed—escalate via IMO weekly update	• IMO process
Subsidiary Suppliers • Ownership change announcement • Any contact changes	• Day 0	• Collect issues thru subsidiary as needed—escalate via IMO weekly update	• IMO process

EXHIBIT 10.9 Communication Planning Audience and Content Planning

of stakeholders. Grouping your audience in this way can help you to focus and refine your messaging as well as the vehicles and feedback loops you need to ensure you are continually optimizing your CMP.

Exhibits 10.8 and 10.9 show how to create matrixed communication plans for each key stakeholder group.

CHAPTER CHECKLIST

Make sure to use the following list of items to check off the most important aspects of a solid communication plan for your integration. Keep in mind the following:

- ☐ Clearly outline communication plan objectives.
- ☐ Establish a communication matrix and tailor key messages for each audience.
- ☐ Plan communication message release dates for at least 90 days.

SUMMARY

In this chapter, we learned how to plan and execute a robust communication plan to support your integration.

Next we will outline some cultural integration topics and how to factor them into your integration planning.

CHAPTER 11

Cultural Integration and Assessment

I n this chapter, you will learn the following:

- Some guiding principles and objectives for managing cultural integration as part of the integration process.
- Assessment guidelines to topics to address when assessing culture.
- The relationship between cultural integration and change management.

Almost every merger involves processes that help to assess and select talent for virtually all levels of an organization. Cultural assessment activities are often overlooked or ignored altogether.

Assessing culture is important as part of a merger or an acquisition. If you think a robust cultural assessment is going to be a considerable undertaking during an integration, it's recommended that you seek advice and support from companies like Pritchett that specialize in this area and have a wealth of experience and tools to help you through the process (see www.pritchettnet.com for more information). Finding additional thought leadership to help shape your plans is money well spent.

It is important that you know enough about cultural integration to recognize when you need help and know how to get it. Cultural clashes are bound to occur on some level with any integration, but if left to fester, they can become a cancer that destroys morale and productivity and can adversely affect business results. So don't underestimate the challenge of integrating cultures between the acquiring company and the company being acquired.

MANAGING CULTURAL INTEGRATION ACTIVITIES

Managing culture and talent activities as part of an integration is handled by the IMO. All of what is outlined here should be undertaken in close partnership with the HR leaders involved in the integration, and getting them in the loop earlier rather than later is a good idea.

To begin, the following offers some guiding principles about culture assessment:

- Cultural assessment tools should be used only when considering a substantial operational integration.
- Cultural assessments inform decision making for IMO planning and need to be completed prior to day 0.

In particular, the specific cultural assessment objectives during an integration can include the following:

- Factoring human due diligence into integration planning.
- Mitigating the adverse effects of cultural dissonance wherever possible.
- Prioritizing issues that may require extra effort and including them in HR and other functional work plans.
- Assessing cultural issues early and following up to update your assessments once the integration work is well underway.

When assessing the issues involved in culturally integrating two companies, there are outstanding tools and processes you can use to help you. As previously mentioned, it is highly recommended that you consult an outside resource (by approaching a firm like Pritchett) if you find yourself with a cultural integration challenge.

Assessing Culture

Exhibits 11.1 through 11.4 offer some abbreviated survey questions to give you an idea of the kinds of issues a robust cultural assessment attempts to diagnose. You should be familiar with most of these areas prior to starting your integration work.

From these assessments, you will find that the benefits of a cultural due diligence process can include the following:

- Raising sensitivity and awareness to issues early so that they can be proactively managed during integration.
- Help in mitigating the effects of taking something away, when necessary (e.g., when acquired employees lose a benefit, perk, or compensation element).
- Stimulating faster resolution of key disagreements that are bogging down integration and/or creating organizational dysfunction.

Strategic Direction	Key Measures & Definition of Results	Structure & Protocols
What is the company's primary value proposition?	What is measured and why?	How is the company organized—by functions, geography, business units?
What are the key business drivers behind the strategy?	How are key measurement categories (customer satisfaction, production, employee satisfaction, etc.) defined?	How do staff and line units relate to each other and get services or deliverables from each other?
What key differentiators does the market recognize?	How are results communicated to external stakeholders and employees?	What degree of customer service perspective exists within staff functions?
What are the key elements of the business plan?	How are these measures linked to rewards and incentives?	How do people access units or resources other than their own?

EXHIBIT 11.1 Assessment Topics: Strategic Direction

Planning & Control Systems	Employee Engagement	Use & Philosophy of IT
What formal systems are in place, and to what extent are they followed?	How widespread are teams or other methods of employee involvement?	What types of technology and architecture currently exist?
Is there more adherence to informal or to formal approaches?	If teams are used, what kinds—for work, special projects, employee relations?	What is the current level of service and compatibility?
What is the company's overall corporate governance process, ethics, and compliance with regulatory requirements?	Is work performed with a primary focus on individual responsibility and accountability or group responsibility?	What are the current issues or concerns with IT?
What degree of consensus or autonomy is typically expected in the formulation of decisions?	Are employees linked to the business plan through processes for goal setting or performance mgmt?	How is technology being used to leverage staff expertise and increase productivity?

EXHIBIT 11.2 Assessment Topics: Planning and Control Systems

Physical Environment	Historical Issues & Expectations	Organization-wide Information Transfer
Is there a dress code?	What major events created and affected the organization?	How readily is info about financial or operating performance disseminated?
Are offices open or private?	What perceptions and obstacles will most employees bring forward?	What is routinely communicated or held back?
What is the look and feel of the offices and plants?	What social activities, special incentives or opportunities, icons or images, etc. may people have a stake in preserving?	To what extent do employees and managers believe that they have access to important information?
What is the impact of the environment on how work gets done?	Are there specific legacies and norms tied to a specific individual?	What types of organization-wide communication channels, programs, and media exist?

EXHIBIT 11.3 Assessment Topics: Physical Environment

Info Transfer between & among Individuals	Leader & Manager Behavior	Human Capital
Is communication between and among individuals and depts. typically more formal or informal?	Are managers selected and rewarded primarily for coaching and facilitative leadership?	How is the HR dept positioned in the org (more like a strategic business partner or administrative unit)?
Are instructions, feedback, and communication given primarily in writing or in person?	What type of boss-subordinate relationship represents the norm?	How able is HR to effect strategic change in the organization?
To ensure fast and effective transfer of information, what types or regularly scheduled meetings exist in the org?	What areas of competence are most predictive of success?	How are benefits provided?
Do employees routinely have access to superiors through an open-door policy?	How are these areas of competence identified, communicated, and developed?	Does the company demonstrate that employees are a valued resource? How?

EXHIBIT 11.4 Assessment Topics: Information Transfer

An initial cultural due diligence assessment can be completed by an integration team through a structured interview process with key executives and the employees of an acquired company. IMO leaders can identify potential cultural issues and recommend strategies to address culture as part of an integration strategy. Some specific IMO duties can include the following:

- Collaborating with division management and corporate HR functions before day 0 to determine the need for a cultural assessment process. Then, if cultural assessment is needed, the IMO ensures that the HR functional work plan includes cultural assessment planning and execution specifics.
- Securing external experts on cultural assessment if needed.
- Driving coordination of the documentation and tracking tools required to manage cultural assessment so the IMO may develop tools for functions as needed.
- Receiving status updates through an IMO weekly process.
- Updating the executive team.
- Coordinating tactical responses to any urgent issues related to cultural assessment initiatives.

Roles and Responsibilities

Exhibit 11.5 shows the various high-level roles and responsibilities in the cultural assessment process. Again, please note that the IMO is responsible for determining the need for cultural assessment. This is a critical deliverable and should be handled with a bias for urgency.

	Role	Accountable For
Integration Management Office	Drives decision making to determine need for cultural assessment processes	Gaining consensus for need and coordinating plan development with HR
Functional Resource Owner (HR)	Manages cultural assessment processes	Ensuring functional resource executes cultural assessment deliverables
Functional Resource	Executes cultural assessment processes	Cultural assessment functional plan completion

EXHIBIT 11.5 Cultural Assessment Process Roles and Responsibilities

	Due Diligence	Integration		End State Monitoring
Goal	Planning & Execution		Monitoring	
When	Pre-Close	First 30 Days	30 – 100 Days	> 100 Days
Activities	• Determine need for cultural assessment (CA) • Finalize stakeholders to be included in CA exercise • Finalize CA questionnaire and specific info needs of division management • Conduct readout of CA assessment and impact to IMO plan with key stakeholders • Integrate CA action items into IMO functional work plans	• Execute first 30 days, functional plans, and CMP plan • Monitor and address feedback	• IMO project status management	• Survey stakeholders to assess CA issues and status

EXHIBIT 11.6   High-level Process/Activities: Cultural Assessment

Activities and the IMO Time Line

Exhibit 11.6 shows cultural assessment activities and when they occur in a typical integration timetable.

It is difficult to get senior executives to acknowledge cultural issues during an integration, so allocate time and resources to make it a priority. Executives often think that these things will "work themselves out," that people will eventually get on board, and that all will be right at the end of the day. Remember, though: It seldom works itself out, and frequently the people you hope will get on board are your highest performers and actually end up getting on board with one of your competitors because you haven't addressed their concerns properly! But it doesn't have to be this way. Spending time understanding the potential cultural issues of your integration and providing senior management with tangible examples of where culture issues will affect integration effectiveness are the keys to success.

Of course, at some point, people do have to get on board—you will never mitigate cultural issues to the satisfaction of all stakeholders. Do your best to prioritize and address the areas that may negatively impact your integration goals and objectives.

CULTURE AND CHANGE MANAGEMENT

Change management is another subject for which experts abound, and there's nothing like a merger to deliver a healthy dose of change to just about everyone involved in a business. Integration leaders need to be considerate of how change affects employees and pay attention to managing that change as part of their integration planning. A few key ways to do this can include the following:

- Addressing the acquired employees' issues quickly.
- Applying defined, clear leadership during change activities.
- Providing extensive communication with acquired employees.
- Ensuring a focus on customers during the change.
- Making tough decisions (quickly and decisively).
- Creating focused initiatives.
- Managing resistance at every level.
- Addressing issues quickly once they arise.

Change can be a tremendously disruptive force, and it must be managed proactively. Change management is another area where there is plenty of consulting expertise to learn from. Therefore, getting assistance from an outside source when it's needed is recommended. As an integration manager, you must stay ahead of the process of change management, factor it into your integration planning, and expect some surprises here and there. People react and internalize change in many different ways, but being ahead of the curve is helpful.

One important aspect of change management is listening. You have to have your ear to the ground to pick up some of the subtle clues that the amount of change is overwhelming some employees and may need to be addressed. Here are some change-fatigue symptoms to be aware of in employees:

- Are they coming to work late, leaving early, or acting slightly disengaged? Is the disengagement resulting in frequent mistakes?
- Do they seem resistant to new ideas and uninterested in new initiatives?
- Do they appear stressed or anxious?
- Are they missing deadlines and performance goals?

Senior leaders can also show signs of change-management fatigue. Here are a few symptoms:

- Are they constantly making requests for change-management communications? This may be a signal that they are trying to fix something over and over again.
- Do they avoid addressing employees directly or do it so infrequently that it's ineffective?

- Do they blame employees for lack of engagement?
- Are they openly showing frustration and want a return to normal or business as usual?

Keep your eyes and ears open so you can spot some of these signs and suggest remedies before it's too late.

Most of all, try to be sensitive to how people, business activities, and customers react to changes when undergoing an integration. Your job is to preserve value and integrate as quickly as possible.

CHAPTER CHECKLIST

Your checklist after reading this chapter includes the following:

- ☐ Establishing cultural integration objectives and guiding principles.
- ☐ Seeking outside help for cultural integration issues when necessary.
- ☐ Addressing change-management issues and learning how to recognize the signs of change fatigue in your organization.

SUMMARY

In this chapter, we learned about cultural integration and how to address and manage culture and change within your integration-planning framework.

Next we will explore how to address the process of talent management in integration execution.

CHAPTER 12

The Talent Assessment Process

I n this chapter you will learn the following:

- The objectives and guiding principles for talent assessment within the integration-planning environment.
- Some tools and tips for managing assessment, retention, and separation activities.

All new organizations need good people in key positions, and talent selection is an important part of any integration plan. Similar to cultural assessments, talent assessments should be done in close conjunction with HR leadership. Companies frequently choose to seek outside experts to help with the specific process elements, given how important assessing talent in an organization can be.

As with any merger, there is always a risk of losing key people, so getting your talent assessment process documented and underway quickly during the first phases of an integration is important. It is typically the people you most want to keep whom you are most at risk of losing. The most talented employees are the ones who have the most options and who likely have headhunters and recruiters reaching out to them as soon as the news of a merger is announced.

TALENT ASSESSMENT GUIDING PRINCIPLES

Talent assessment processes are often accompanied by some specific retention plans from the HR manager. Getting these activities done expediently is of the utmost importance.

After you have gotten a process set up, here are some additional guidelines on managing talent-related integration activities from the IMO:

- Talent assessment tools can be used for functional and operational integrations when position duplication or staff-reduction requirements warrant a systematic approach to personnel evaluation. Remember that the assessment tools and criteria in this chapter are for general business use. They will require customization by HR to align with the specific business objectives and talent criteria of a particular integration and the newco organization or acquiring company.
- The retention and separation tools offered here are also for general business use and require customization by the legal and HR departments to align with the corporate policy in your integration. These processes should be completed within 30 to 45 days of day 0 for optimal results.

TALENT ASSESSMENT OBJECTIVES

Talent assessment objectives can include the following:

- Identifying key talent from the acquired subsidiary employee base.
- Facilitating efficient background and performance verification.
- Creating a consistent evaluation process.

The best approach to making position selection during a merger or an acquisition is to institute a uniform and consistent approach and to include all levels of the organization. Since most senior leaders are almost always defined soon after closing day, talent assessment can typically include an approach that specifies a range of positions (e.g., from the senior vice president on down). Even if some incumbents are considered lock-ins for their positions or the combined new positions, going through the assessment process sends the message that senior leadership is evaluating all options and is being objective.

When talent assessment is applied sporadically or inconsistently, it can send the message that management is selectively moving people out or is disorganized. Any experienced and successful HR professional will tell you that doing spotty assessments is improper and can lead to unforeseen consequences down the road. Therefore, if you are going to undertake a talent assessment process, make sure it is applied uniformly and consistently and within a specified time frame.

Exhibit 12.1 shows the high-level roles and responsibilities for assessing talent during an integration.

	Due Diligence	Integration	End State Monitoring
Goal	Planning & Execution		Monitoring	
When	Pre-Close	First 30 Days	30 – 100 Days	> 100 Days
Activities	• Determine need for talent assessment (TA) • Finalize stakeholders to be included in TA exercise • Finalize TA criteria and specific needs of division management • Integrate TA process into HR functional work plan	• Execute as part of HR functional plan	• Execute as part of HR functional plan	• End state tracking as needed

EXHIBIT 12.1   Talent Assessment High-level Process/Activities

EVALUATION TOOLS FOR ASSESSING TALENT

Below are some very simple guidelines to inform your thinking on what the best talent assessment tools and criteria would be for your particular integration. The assessment criteria for your industry and organization might be different from what is included here, so remember to work with your senior management and HR leaders to create the criteria and tools that best suit the needs of your new organization.

At the highest level, you should develop executive selection criteria in conjunction with HR. Exhibit 12.2 shows a simple approach to use for that purpose; it is a simple diagram outlining how a specific company's specified criteria needed to contribute to growth (which is a key objective of the company shown, as for almost every company).

It is important to create an approach similar to the one in Exhibit 12.2 so you have a context for your evaluation. If you're not sure what is going to be important in the new organization in terms of talent, skills, and values, it will be pretty difficult to make objective decisions about what kind of people will make good leaders down the road.

Next, define the values for each criterion (see Exhibit 12.3).

After you've defined your general criteria, it is important to define the specific criteria in a little more detail. You can reach out to senior leaders and HR to help decide what should go in each of these areas. With the involvement of key leaders in different departments, talent assessment is also a catalyst for robust discussions about key planning dimensions of the new organization.

Exhibits 12.4 and 12.5 show specific indicators and behaviors for each of the key criteria outlined in Exhibit 12.3.

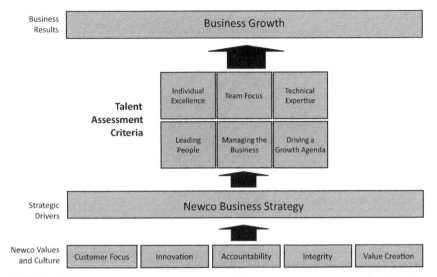

EXHIBIT 12.2   How Talent Assessment Criteria Contributes to Business Growth

Breaking up your talent assessment activities into key phases is highly recommended. It is also highly likely that you will need to incorporate senior leadership reviews at key points in the process of developing the assessment criteria.

RETENTION AND SEPARATION GUIDELINES AND POLICIES

Exhibit 12.6 shows a typical process flow for talent assessment. For the purposes of illustration, the terms *divisions* and *GM* are used, but your organization structure will most likely be different.

Unfortunately, it is often necessary to separate some people from the organization for a variety of reasons. Head count and full-time equivalent (FTE) reductions are most always a big part of the synergy savings forecast. Many times the IMO will manage the retention and separation process as part of its integration duties.

There are some guidelines and basic rules to make this a dignified and professional process, and, as always, HR should be in lockstep with the IMO and department leaders during all parts of this process. Also, remember to make decisions quickly and communicate when decisions will be made. The longer the employees wait around wondering if they have jobs, the less

Criteria	Indicators	Behaviors
Leading People	Possesses Clear Vision	• Possesses a clear vision for the future and conveys a view of how things could be different • Develops strategies and short- and long-term plans for translating vision into reality
	Builds Strong Teams	• Considers employees' strengths and weaknesses when assembling teams (while also sourcing quality talent) • Makes assignments and promotions on the basis of ability and not politics and friendship
	Drives Performance	• Provides clear direction and priorities; clarifies team member roles and responsibilities • Provides frequent, timely, and accurate performance feedback and makes tough decisions
	Encourages & Inspires	• Builds a sense of unity and purpose among team members through motivational leadership and setting common goals and objectives • Empowers subordinates and gives them room to do their jobs
Driving a Growth Agenda	Is Innovative & Creative	• Combines perspectives and approaches in creative ways and makes connections between seemingly unrelated ideas; also encourages this behavior in others • Anticipates and delivers innovative solutions that meet or exceed customer expectations
	Embraces Change	• Monitors and communicates changes in the marketplace and business environment • Responds quickly and effectively to changing situations or unanticipated problems
	Is Entrepreneurial	• Generates breakthrough ideas for growing the business (new products, new business opportunities) • Makes bold moves and takes calculated risk (chooses to invest in new markets, products, processes, and partnerships)
	Is Execution Focused	• Translates innovative/entrepreneurial ideas into tangible programs that are easy to support and implement • Manages day-to-day business requirements effectively

EXHIBIT 12.3 Talent Assessment Criteria: Leading People; Driving a Growth Agenda

Criteria	Indicators	Behaviors
Managing the Business	Creates Value	• Creates economic and shareholder value by contributing to sustainable business solutions and products and understands and acts on the business drivers
	Seeks Business Opportunities	• Embraces organizational constraints and uses to advantage • Translates external opportunities into value for the business
	Is Customer Focused	• Always acts with the customer in mind; keeps employees abreast of customer needs • Works hard to intimately understand customers' needs
	Is Action Oriented	• Demonstrates enthusiasm, drive, rigor, and a sense of urgency when managing the business • Leads continuous improvement initiatives; streamlines processes and adopts innovative practices
Team Focus	Demonstrates Global Understanding	• Takes a global perspective when planning strategy and making decisions • Brings diverse talent together when establishing teams and allows and encourages the movement and growth of talented individuals
	Collaborates	• Promotes collaboration and cross-functional sharing and integration among team members and colleagues • Encourages open discussion of ideas and opinions
	Builds Effective Relationships	• Creates positive working relationships with team members, peers, and management, both within and outside own business unit and division • Easily develops rapport with a wide range of personalities; quickly gains trust and credibility • Builds strong internal and external networks to create business opportunities

EXHIBIT 12.4 Talent Assessment Criteria: Managing the Business; Team Focus

Criteria	Indicators	Behaviors
Individual Excellence	Accountable	• Is open, forthright, and truthful; demonstrates consistency in words and actions • Keeps promises with no excuses; meets deadlines and delivers within budget
	Personal Integrity	• Embodies company values and lets these guide decision making and behavior • Conducts business ethically; expects others to do the same • Treats all individuals fairly and with respect and dignity
	Performance-Oriented	• Consistently strives for success and achieves superior results • Is productive, creates value, and makes an impact
	Personal Resilience	• Sustains a high level of energy and a positive attitude in the face of difficult challenges or adversity • Manages emotional reactions and maintains composure
Technical Expertise	Learning Agility	• Easily grasps the essence and the underlying structure of anything; learns quickly when facing new problems and situations • Applies existing knowledge to different situations and changing circumstances
	Analytical Thinking	• Cuts through complexity to achieve clarity about what is important • Dissects complex problems and is able to make connections and link key issues
	Focused Results	• Delivers key short-term and long-term objectives • Utilizes relevant financial information to help guide strategy; monitors budgets and achieves appropriate financial goals for the business/function • Uses business processes and knowledge to achieve results

EXHIBIT 12.5 Talent Assessment Criteria: Individual Excellence; Technical Expertise

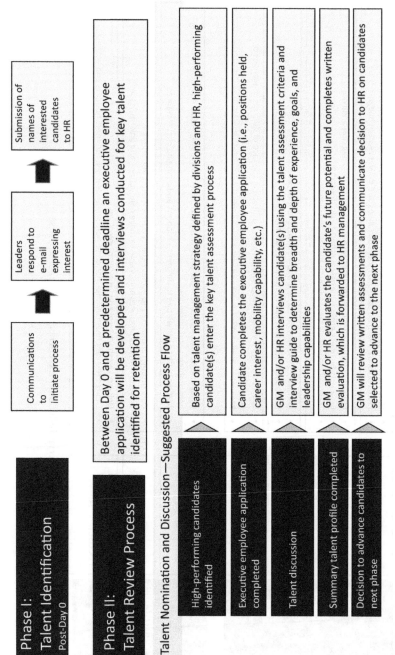

Phase I:
Talent Identification
Post–Day 0

Communications to initiate process

Leaders respond to e-mail expressing interest

Submission of names of interested candidates to HR

Phase II:
Talent Review Process

Between Day 0 and a predetermined deadline an executive employee application will be developed and interviews conducted for key talent identified for retention

Talent Nomination and Discussion—Suggested Process Flow

High-performing candidates identified → Based on talent management strategy defined by divisions and HR, high-performing candidate(s) enter the key talent assessment process

Executive employee application completed → Candidate completes the executive employee application (i.e., positions held, career interest, mobility capability, etc.)

Talent discussion → GM and/or HR interviews candidate(s) using the talent assessment criteria and interview guide to determine breadth and depth of experience, goals, and leadership capabilities

Summary talent profile completed → GM and/or HR evaluates the candidate's future potential and completes written evaluation, which is forwarded to HR management

Decision to advance candidates to next phase → GM will review written assessments and communicate decision to HR on candidates selected to advance to the next phase

EXHIBIT 12.6 Talent Assessment: Process Example

productive they get. Uncertainty is the number one productivity killer post-merger, so eliminate the potential risk by being proactive and communicating selection timing. HR may often need to update policies or craft new ones, given the scope of a separation project. The worst thing that can happen is for those affected to feel that the process and tools were half-baked or inconsistently applied.

It is recommended that you review the HR process yourself and ask, "How would I expect to be treated in this situation?" Then execute separations in waves and on the same day. It is best to group separation decisions and affected individuals so that this activity is done all at once. For example, alert the following:

- Vice presidents and above by X date
- Directors by X date
- Managers by X date
- All others by X date

Having your communications timed and organized accomplishes the following:

- It enables those named to be involved in the selection of their respective organizations and teams.
- It creates a timetable you can use for communication purposes.
- It allows the process to unfold within a rational and realistic time frame.

DEPENDENCIES FOR TALENT ASSESSMENT AND RETENTION AND SEPARATION ACTIVITIES

The timing of assessment, retention, and separation activities is often in direct conflict with the integration work you are trying to accomplish. For example, you're trying to get all this integration work done, and people are leaving or are not officially in their new roles yet. Perhaps they are even in limbo and have not yet landed in a specific role in the new organization.

Here are a few common scenarios along with some suggestions on how best to manage these fluid situations. Once again, it is always best to work with your HR manager to develop the solution that serves the needs of the integration but is also in alignment with HR policies and guidelines.

Note that IT is the example function in the scenarios outlined here, and these situations could apply to nearly any function.

Example Scenario 1

Problem: The IT integration work streams are defined, but the IT organization has not settled on its structure and personnel yet, so there's no one assigned to do the work.

There are a couple of ways to handle this issue:

1. Ask the senior leadership of the IT organization to assign a temporary manager to the integration work that has been defined. Even if the person is only temporarily assigned to the IMO, you can at least make some progress on the integration work, and you will have a direct link to the IT organization for prioritizing issues and getting any urgent questions answered.
2. See if you can push the IT work streams back a bit so they align with the starting date of your dedicated resource. Implement this carefully, however, in order to make sure any delays do not compromise other integration work streams. Be sure you are aware of any critical cross-functional dependencies before agreeing to any date changes.

Example Scenario 2

Problem: The IT personnel assigned to the integration are temporary in the sense that they do not yet know whether they will be part of the new organization.

This is one of the most difficult situations because people who are unsure whether they have a place in the new organization are distracted and are focused on finding a permanent position more than on doing integration work. All this is understandable, but the work still has to get done.

Therefore, the best solution here is to remind the affected person that performing well in an integration capacity is a sure way to help his or her own cause and that a strong showing in an important albeit temporary role is a good way to get noticed by senior management. It sounds a bit self-serving for the IMO, but it is far better for the person to be generating a positive performance record while in limbo because it could affect some decision making and work to that person's advantage.

Example Scenario 3

Problem: The talent assessment has been completed, and the poor performers have been assigned to the IMO.

Believe it or not, this happens quite frequently. After performance reviews are completed, instead of separating poor performers, senior leaders assign them to the IMO. They can't bear to fire anybody and may be hoping that the person has a metamorphosis and magically turns into an exceptional performer.

Either way, it is a problem for the integration leader, since having poor performers assigned to functional work streams is not ideal and also taints others working on the integration. In addition, it increases the perception that the IMO is a way station for poor performers.

Integration teams should include your best and brightest, so here are two solutions if you run into the problem:

1. *Push back.* Meet with the senior leadership of that function and discuss options. Be discreet and respectful, but make sure you communicate that you need a strong performer, not an individual who may not make the cut.
2. *Delay the work stream.* If the affected person is truly on the way out, sometimes it may be best to just hold off on commencing the work streams until a new person can be assigned. Make sure you are aware of any critical cross-functional dependencies before making any decisions to delay integration work. Once again, all of these decisions should be made in partnership with HR.

THINGS TO AVOID

Don't let human resources or anyone else rush the talent assessment process because a synergy time line is tied to separating employees by a certain date. A couple of days here or there won't make a huge difference. The damage done by a poorly executed separation process is permanent, and all those affected are likely to bad-mouth the new company. Word can get around to your customers and cause unneeded public relations problems. Integrations are difficult enough without having to address public relations flare-ups. Also keep in mind that social media can let disgruntled employees vent publicly for the whole world to see. Treat people as well as you can during this tender period in a newly merged company.

On rare occasions, getting security to walk someone out the door is prudent. In most cases, however, it is completely unnecessary, and so are plans to have security present as people clean out their desks. This type of treatment is demeaning in general and a mistake in most cases. Try not to make the event more painful than it already is by making it a show. Use common sense and remember that for most people, this is one of the most difficult things they will ever experience.

	Due Diligence		Integration	End State Monitoring
Goal	Planning & Execution			Monitoring
When	Pre-Close	First 30 Days	30 – 100 Days	> 100 Days
Activities	•Determine if synergy plan requires subsidiary head-count reductions •Finalize what functional parties and acquired executives will be involved in •Retention/separation (R/S) planning •Finalize R/S planning worksheets and begin collecting data (part of HR functional work plan) •Draft separation and retention agreements and documents (HR) and run thru legal	•Execute R/S process as part of HR functional plan	•Begin LDW (last day worked) tracking as part of HR functional plan	•End state and LDW tracking as needed

EXHIBIT 12.7   High-level Process/Activities—Retention/Separation Planning

Exhibit 12.7 provides some guidance for employee separation and retention processes as part of a successful integration plan.

CHAPTER CHECKLIST

Your checklist for this chapter includes the following:

☐ Establish specific objectives and guiding principles for talent assessment prior to starting any work in this area.
☐ Create tools and templates in conjunction with HR to ensure consistency.

SUMMARY

In this chapter, we learned how to manage talent assessment activities within the framework of integration planning.

Next we will outline some tips and tools for synergy program management.

CHAPTER **13**

Synergy Program Management

I n this chapter you will learn the following:

- What activities define synergy.
- How to manage synergy programs within the IMO framework.
- How to use some simple tools and templates for tracking and reporting synergies.

Almost every merger or acquisition includes cost savings and business benefits arising from synergies (essentially, positive business outcomes as a result of the merger). Synergies can take many forms: employee reductions, revenue enhancements, plant rationalizations, store closings, purchasing optimization, and much more. The list can be quite extensive, and synergies are typically the number one driver of the merger or acquisition.

IMOs are seldom responsible for generating original synergy projections, but they are almost always involved in helping to manage synergy program realizations. Setting up a robust platform to help realize synergies is a critical IMO deliverable and one that should be carefully managed. You could do everything else right, but failing here would result in the IMO being perceived as underdelivering on its overall integration objectives.

A synergy is a cost savings or a revenue increase that the combined companies would not have achieved as stand-alone companies. Synergies result primarily from the following opportunities:

- Increased scale of the combined companies.
- Labor cost (internal and third-party) reductions as a result of overlapping functions, efficiencies of scale, or process improvement from the adoption of best practices from both legacy companies.
- Elimination of overlapping and redundant spending, including supplier spending (e.g., marketing costs, warehousing, shipping, and IT services).

127

- Cost avoidance for planned capacity upgrades (e.g., by increasing utilization of the combined capabilities of the two companies, like warehouse expansion plans).
- Cross-selling or up-selling opportunities.

Conversely, the following are not synergies:

- Volume-driven variances without the above criteria (e.g., lower sales driving lower supply costs).
- Operating improvements that would have occurred regardless of the acquisition integration.

Unfortunately, industry experts from a variety of sources are quick to point out that the majority of mergers fail to deliver fully on synergy forecasts. The number usually given can range from 50 to 70 percent of mergers failing to achieve the projected synergy forecasts. This failure can be caused by a variety of factors, including inflated synergy forecasts, changing market conditions (e.g., projected cost savings affected because of an increase in the price of a raw material), or poor tracking and program management.

EFFECTIVELY MANAGING SYNERGIES

To take advantage of synergies, you need to put detailed plans in place to manage cost-reduction or revenue-enhancement activities to ensure they occur on time and deliver the projected result. Good synergy tracking and management as part of post-merger integration can help you to keep your integration plan on track. Here's how your IMO should support synergy tracking and objectives:

- Provide the processes and tools for achieving the planned synergy benefits.
- Identify the participants in the process and their roles and responsibilities.
- Capture the synergy opportunity concepts that were identified before the closing.
- Work with the business division and acquired company's management leaders to evolve concepts into actionable plans, including the following:
  - Approach
  - Schedule
  - Accountable owner
  - Defined and scheduled benefit measurement approaches

An additional key to evolving the initial concepts into an actionable plan is for the owner (the person or function responsible for the synergy) to be engaged in the definition of approach, schedule, benefit measurement methodology, investments required, and trade-off versus other opportunity costs and program management.

Guiding principles of effective synergy programs during an integration include the following:

- Assigning accountable owners and then committing to a plan and doing the proper follow-up; otherwise initiatives will be deprioritized.
- Making sure that planned deal benefits that require further analysis by assigned accountable owners in order to achieve buy-ins are reviewed and revisited.
- Following up on agreements on planned measurement approaches and their timing.
- Ensuring that initiatives are supported and linked to integration-related projects.
- Motivating through existing employee performance assessment and incentives within the organization whenever possible. This includes putting special incentives in place when required.
- Not overmeasuring or losing focus on key operational measurements.
- Approaching needs to systematically manage changes to the baseline, including additional discovery, which may reveal more or less opportunity.
- Shifting benefits and costs between functional owners, if necessary.
- Reevaluating the benefits and costs because of changes in the market.
- Managing cross-functionally to ensure that costs are not simply shifted to other parts of the business.

THE IMO'S ROLE IN MANAGING A SYNERGY PROGRAM

As with the integration project portfolio, the IMO manages the development of individual synergy initiative plans by the initiative owners. IMO duties can include the following:

- Planning schedules.
- Integrating components into summary views.
- Driving project-sponsor approvals of baseline plans.
- Facilitating cross-functional negotiations and decisions for synergy initiatives that have a cross-functional opportunity or effect.

	Due Diligence	Integration		End State Monitoring
Goal	Planning and Execution		Feedback & Optimization	
When	Pre-Close	First 30 Days	30 – 100 Days	> 100 Days

Activities	• Identify potential synergy opportunities from due diligence
	• Assemble integration team
	• Assign accountable owners to plan synergy initiatives:
	  • Option analysis
	  • Benefits/costs
	  • Timing
	  • Measurement method
		• Complete synergy initiative analysis
		• Ensure initiatives are supported by a project plan
		• Ensure buy-in from accountable owner
		• Achieve fiscal approval for any investments (cost to achieve)
			• Initiate/execute synergy initiative plans
			• Monitor & control projects using project management tools
			• Periodically measure and report synergy achievement results
			• Use change-management process to systematically manage change
				• Transition synergy reporting to become part of normal operational review processes (e.g., subsidiary quarterly review)

EXHIBIT 13.1   SMP High-level Process/Activities

- Owning the change-management process and facilitating approvals from project sponsors.
- Receiving synergy initiative updates from owners through a periodic template.
- Updating executive team members on program progress.

Exhibit 13.1 shows typical synergy management–plan activities at key stages of integration.

Sometimes another firm specializing in cost-reduction activities is responsible for the bulk of the synergy management activities. In that case, it is important to clarify what the IMO is responsible for and what it is not. Typically, the tracking and reporting of synergies is managed as a separate activity within finance or operations when another firm is responsible. If the IMO is responsible for all or part of synergy program management, Exhibit 13.2 shows the IMO and functional owner roles in the process. It also shows a more detailed synergy accountability breakdown.

A TYPICAL SYNERGY PLAN

Exhibits 13.3 and 13.4 give an idea of the kind of content one might find in a typical synergy plan. There are dozens of online and program management tools available to track synergy plans, and it's recommended that you explore collaborative software reporting tools like Daptiv and Inchieve for such needs.

	Role	Accountable For
Integration Management Office	Overall program management of synergy initiatives: plans development, execution, and monitoring and controlling	• Synergy initiative assignments • Driving planning process • Integrating individual initiatives into one baseline • Managing cross-functional facilitation/decisions • Getting baseline approved by project sponsor • Driving change-management process
Synergy Initiative Owner	• Defines, plans, and achieves synergy initiative benefits • Reviews and drives internal fiscal approval of any investments	• Achieving benefits within planned costs and schedule • Allocating resources to define, plan, and achieve synergy benefits
Accounting Resources	• Defines and implements measurement of benefits and costs • Establishes tracking cost accounts if required • Ensures costs tie to appropriate general ledger items (e.g., integration costs) • Maintains any supporting documentation if required	• Periodically report benefits achievement vs. plan via synergy tracking templates • Ensuring accuracy of any accounting impacts

EXHIBIT 13.2 Synergy Program Management Roles and Responsibilities

At its most basic level, synergy reporting should include the following:

A Periodic (Quarterly or Monthly) Executive Review

- It summarizes synergy initiative statuses for key initiatives and both on and off track for whole plans.
- It facilitates plan, issue, and baseline change discussions.

A Master Synergy Plan

- It provides a macro view of performance versus the overall plan.
- It includes dependencies between project portfolio elements and synergy initiatives.
- It links to initiative templates.

Accountability

- Each synergy initiative has an accountable owner, and accounting support for that owner periodically updates progress in a template.
- There is one tracking template per initiative.

SYNERGY PLANNING	
Capture those synergy opportunities identified by deal team	IMO
Assign synergy opportunities for analysis by functional owners:	Functional owner
- Identify achievable amounts	
- Identify achievable schedule	Division/subsidiary lead
- Accountable owner	
- Measurement methodology	
Manage cross-functional collaboration required to decide how and in what function integration benefits can be achieved	IMO
Integrate synergy initiative opportunities into overall baseline plan:	IMO
- Total opportunity	
- Measurement method	
- Achievement timing	
- Accountable initiative owners	
- Linkage to project in integration project portfolio	
Attain project-sponsor approval for baseline	IMO
MONITORING & CONTROLLING	
Customize/distribute synergy reporting templates	IMO
Periodically (monthly, quarterly) complete synergy reporting templates	Functional owner/accounting support
Ensure integration costs are captured in appropriate cost accounts (e.g., one-time integration vs. operational expense)	Accounting support
Ensure projects that drive the synergies remain on track	Functional owner
MANAGING CHANGE	
Evaluate functional owners' requests to change baseline due to:	IMO
- Detailed discovery has revealed more/less benefit	
- Operational changes in the business have impacted the planned benefits	
- A better approach to achievement has been developed but requires benefit/cost allocation changes between functions	
Attain project-sponsor approval for changes to baseline	IMO
END STATE TRANSITION	
Ensure reporting for long-duration synergy initiatives have:	IMO
- Assigned accountable owner	
- Incorporated into normal operational reporting	

EXHIBIT 13.3 Synergy Work-Plan Example

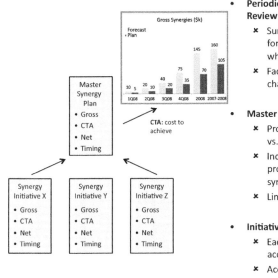

- **Periodic (Quarterly/Monthly) Executive Review**
  - ✗ Summarizes synergy initiative status for key initiatives and on/off track for whole plan
  - ✗ Facilitates plan, issue, and baseline change discussions

- **Master Synergy Plan**
  - ✗ Provides macro view to performance vs. plan
  - ✗ Includes dependencies between project portfolio elements and synergy initiatives
  - ✗ Links to initiative templates

- **Initiative Level**
  - ✗ Each synergy initiative has an accountable owner
  - ✗ Accounting support for that owner periodically updates template
  - ✗ One Excel template per initiative

EXHIBIT 13.4 Synergy Reporting Structure

Process Details

The synergy tracking templates shown in Exhibits 13.5, 13.6, and 13.7 should be used for inspiration only, because whatever tracking tools you need should be developed in conjunction with senior management and your finance teams.

Exhibit 13.5 is a standard initiative input tracker, Exhibit 13.6 shows the financial modeling projected out by year, and Exhibit 13.7 shows an executive summary of gross synergy, costs to achieve (CTA), and net synergy.

Costs to Achieve

Costs to achieve (CTAs) are any expenses incurred as a result of capturing a planned synergy. These need to be estimated along with the synergy forecasts so you can arrive at a net synergy forecast.

Many synergy plans have been subverted by poor or incomplete CTA forecasting, so it is important to be diligent and check these with your finance teams to make sure yours are sound.

Initiative Input Sheet

PLEASE FILL OUT ONLY CELLS SHADED YELLOW

#		
1	Functional Team Name:	Chemical Division: Newco Project Team
2	Synergy Initiative Number:	001
3	Initiative Name:	Cross-Utilization Synergies
		Company A and Company B manufacture very different water-based adhesives and an investment would be necessary to utilize this facility and support Company B's customers on the West Coast.
		Measurable Synergy Benefits:
		- Lowered transport costs
		- Reduced inventory to support JIT locally
		Intangibles:
		- Improved customer service responsiveness
4	Initiative Description:	
		An investment of $200k for new equipment and an additional operator would be needed to support Company B's acrylic and polyurethane dispersion water-based adhesives for its current customers.
5	Cost to Achieve Description:	
6	Cost to Achieve Code:	Cost Account #
7	Does the initiative involve decommissioning an asset:	No
8	If yes, is the asset owned or leased?	Yes
9	Integration Project Dependency/Link	Describe
10	Initiative Implementation Owner:	Chemical Division: Name
11	Cost Center:	TDB
12	Team Lead:	Add team lead names here
13	Team Lead Sign-Off (Accountable Owner, Functional Resource Manager):	Yes

EXHIBIT 13.5 Synergy Initiative Tracking Sheet Example

Other Team Input

Assumptions/Calculations

A	Baseline amount available for synergy benefit	200 tons
B	Averge number of miles saved per quarter tan	1,000 miles
C	Price/tan/mile	$ 0.30
D	Assumed increase/decrease in amount per quarter	1% anticipate increased sales due to customers penetration of Z market
E	Additional operator per quarter (loaded rate)	$17,500.00
F	Cart of equipment required to implement change	$200,000.00

	Q1 2010	Q2 2010	Q3 2010	Q4 2010	Q1 2011	Q2 2011	Q3 2011	Q4 2011	Q1 2012	Q2 2012	Q3 2012	Q4 2012	TOTAL
Synergy Contributions													
Reduced Shipping Cost Benefits	$60,000	$60,600	$61,206	$61,818	$62,436	$63,061	$63,691	$64,328	$64,971	$65,621	$66,277	$66,940	$760,950
Inventory Carrying Cost Savings	$0	$0	$0	$0	$0	$0	$0	$0	$0	$0	$0	$0	$0
TOTAL	$60,000	$60,600	$61,206	$61,818	$62,436	$63,061	$63,691	$64,328	$64,971	$65,621	$66,277	$66,940	$760,950
Costs to Achieve													
Equipment Investment	$200,000	$0	$0	$0	$0	$0	$0	$0	$0	$0	$0	$0	$200,000
Other Project Costs	$80,000	$0	$0	$0	$0	$0	$0	$0	$0	$0	$0	$0	$80,000
Order Process Management Training	$10,000	$0	$0	$0	$0	$0	$0	$0	$0	$0	$0	$0	$10,000
Incremental Sustaining Head Count (TBD)	$17,500	$17,500	$17,500	$17,500	$17,500	$17,500	$17,500	$17,500	$17,500	$17,500	$17,500	$17,500	$210,000
TOTAL	$307,500	$17,500	$17,500	$17,500	$17,500	$17,500	$17,500	$17,500	$17,500	$17,500	$17,500	$17,500	$500,000
Net Synergies	-$247,500	$43,100	$43,706	$44,318	$44,936	$45,561	$46,191	$46,828	$47,471	$48,121	$48,777	$49,440	$260,950

EXHIBIT 13.6 Synergy Forecast Example

	Gross Synergy		Cost to Achieve		Net	
	1Q10 Forecast	1Q10 Plan Var	1Q10 Forecast	1Q10 Plan Var	1Q10 Forecast	1Q10 Plan Var
EBITDA Synergies						
Cross-utilization	42,500	-	90,000	90,000	(47,500)	(47,500)
Synergy Initiative 2	-	-	-	-	-	-
Synergy Initiative 3	-	-	-	-	-	-
Synergy Initiative 4	-	-	-	-	-	-
Synergy Initiative 5	-	-	-	-	-	-
Other Shared Services	-	-	-	-	-	-
EBITDA	42,500	-	90,000	90,000	(47,500)	(47,500)
Capex Synergies						
Cross-utilization	-	-	200,000	200,000	(200,000)	(200,000)
Synergy Initiative 2	-	-	-	-	-	-
Synergy Initiative 3	-	-	-	-	-	-
Synergy Initiative 6	-	-	-	-	-	-
Synergy Initiative 7	-	-	-	-	-	-
Total Capex	-	-	-	-	-	-
Working Capital/Other	-	-	-	-	-	-
Total Synergies	-	-	200,000	200,000	(200,000)	(200,000)

EXHIBIT 13.7 Synergy Forecast Example

BEST PRACTICES

Avoiding synergy busts is important. You can employ some of the strategies and tactics outlined in this chapter, but note that effective synergy program management involves many parties in addition to the IMO.

Managing the Handoff

If there's a due diligence or consulting firm responsible for the bulk of the synergy plan, make sure you have at least one or two handoff meetings so the IMO can get a comprehensive download on the synergy plan. Understanding the rationale and business assumptions behind the plan gives you some added perspective.

Defining the Undefined

Sometimes the synergy plan includes a bunch of yet undefined synergies. For example, nonlabor synergies may refer to all synergies that are not in the head-count bunch. While this is common, it is difficult for the IMO to help manage and track this bunch until it is more defined. Specifically, the bunch needs to be broken down into specific projects (e.g., purchasing consolidation or waste-management vendor consolidation). Don't accept responsibility for tracking these synergies until they are better defined and accountability is assigned.

Delays Almost Always Negatively Affect Synergies

It is best to assume that any delay to a synergy program work stream will negatively affect the attainment of that synergy goal. For example, if there are specific head-count reductions that have to be effective by a specified date, then any delay in separating those employees by the specified date negatively affects the synergy forecast. Every week those employees are on the payroll is a cost incurred instead of a savings.

Bad News Does Not Get Better with Age

If you are in the middle of your integration and see some potential synergy problems developing, raise the red flag right away. Granted, the owner of that particular work stream might not appreciate the attention, but at least it will give executives a chance to right the issue before it becomes a bona fide synergy bust. Once a synergy opportunity is delayed, it is pretty much compromised for good.

If It Looks Too Good to Be True, It Probably Is

There are some amazingly optimistic synergy planning assumptions that can arise when a deal is cut, so sometimes it is necessary to gut-check some of these assumptions to see if they are truly realistic. One of my favorite examples here is cross-selling, in which newly combined companies will now sell each other's products. Sounds reasonable, but there are a few things that have to transpire to make this a reality:

- Salespeople have to be trained to sell the new products.
- Commission systems have to be updated to make sure the salespeople get paid for selling the new products.
- Marketing has to provide the sales force with the tools to sell an aggregated product portfolio.

There are many things to do before cross-selling becomes a reality. Cross-selling benefits frequently appear soon after day one, as though all of the above were going to get done instantly!

Give some of these synergy planning programs a stress test to root out potential wishful thinking while you work with various program owners to outline the most realistic plans and time frames.

CHAPTER CHECKLIST

Your checklist for this chapter includes the following:

- ☐ Guiding principles for effective synergy program management.
- ☐ The IMO's role in the synergy program management process.
- ☐ Tools, templates, and process tips.
- ☐ Lessons learned for effective synergy program management.

SUMMARY

In this chapter, we learned about basic tools, templates, and tips to help you with synergy program management.

Next we will explore some basic guidelines for managing IT integrations.

CHAPTER 14

Information Technology Integration

Matthew Podowitz

*T*his chapter, addressing the IT aspects of a post-merger integration process, is authored by my friend and colleague Matt Podowitz. I asked Matt
to contribute his knowledge and expertise on this topic because of his unique
take on the role of IT in creating value during an integration. Matt has also
developed, and graciously shared here, several simple but innovative and
effective approaches and tools he has developed to help companies direct
and empower their IT functions to do just that.

Matt has served as a strategic compliance, operations, technology, and
transactions advisor for boards and executives at more than 100 companies.
In his almost 20 years of transaction experience, Matt has led operations
and technology due diligence, post-merger planning, or integration efforts
on more than 300 M&A transactions. He is also an accomplished writer
and speaker on operations and technology value creation topics and has
authored or has been featured in articles regarding operations cost reduction,
technology strategy, and post-merger integration in CIO magazine, BizTech
magazine, and in the online editions of Business News Daily, Information
Week, the Wall Street Journal, and other leading news outlets.

Matt's focus always begins and ends with value creation, and this has
been a primary focus of all his efforts to help his clients successfully integrate
companies. Many companies approach IT as just another department to be
integrated. Matt helps companies both to successfully integrate IT departments and to leverage the inherent capabilities and resources of companies'
IT to improve the process and outcomes of the overall integration. Here
he shares several straightforward but effective approaches, as well as some
tools to help implement them.

*   *   *

In this chapter, you will learn the following:

- The role of IT in integration planning.
- IT planning for day one.
- The most common IT integration risks.

As the use of IT in business has become ever more pervasive, so has its importance in planning and executing a successful integration. In fact, a 2011 *McKinsey Quarterly* article shared the results of a study indicating that more than half of the potential synergies in an integration are related to or directly dependent upon IT.[*] However, IT typically receives little priority during the due diligence process or even during integration planning prior to a transaction closing.

This lack of priority, and the associated tendency to involve IT executives in the due diligence and integration planning, creates three key challenges during the integration itself:

- The potential savings to result from integrating IT functions may not be as great, or realized as quickly, as set out in the investment thesis.
- Potential operational synergies or savings in the investment thesis that are dependent on IT may not be plausible, as great, or as quickly realized.
- Significant opportunities to realize even greater or quicker savings or synergies than those posited in the investment thesis may go undiscovered or unrealized.

These challenges and their underlying causes most often stem from a perception of IT as a vertical function or a department within an enterprise and not also a foundation on which every other vertical function or department in the enterprise is built.

IT'S ROLE WITHIN AN INTEGRATION

Exhibit 14.1 shows the two distinct roles of IT within an integration: as a vertical department to be integrated and as a foundation for the integration of other vertical departments.

---

[*]Hugo Sarrazin and Adam West, "Understanding the Strategic Value of IT in M&A," *McKinsey Quarterly*, January 2011.

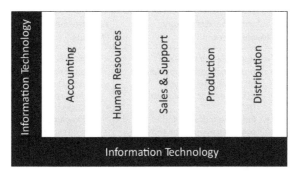

EXHIBIT 14.1   Roles of IT within an Integration

To enhance the potential for savings, synergies, and the overall success of an integration, it is critical for IT to be considered as early as possible in the life cycle of an integration transaction. While doing so often runs counter to the culture of many enterprises, it is a key driver in the success of many integration efforts.

Exhibits 14.2 to 14.4 show the optimal involvement and focus of an enterprise's IT function in the earliest stages of an integration transaction.

Many enterprises and their IT leaders struggle with how to best define and quantify the expected role and impact of IT when planning an integration. This often arises as a result of driving IT integration planning from the perspective of specific IT changes to be made (people, process, and technology) rather than starting with the investment thesis. Working from the

Transaction Phase	Information Technology Involvement	Key Information Technology Outputs
Pre-Letter of Intent (Investment Thesis)	• Development and defense of investment thesis • Information technology synergy identification and quantification • Subject-matter input into non-information technology identification and quantification • Development of due diligence focus areas	• Realistic and achievable synergies resulting from integration of information technology departments • Potential synergies (or roadblocks to synergies) elsewhere in the business that are dependent upon information technology • Straw-case estimates of labor and capital required to realize the synergies outlines in the investment thesis • Key assumptions with regard to potential synergies and cost estimates

EXHIBIT 14.2   IT Involvement and Focus: Pre-Letter Phase

Transaction Phase	Information Technology Involvement	Key Information Technology Outputs
Pre-Signing (Due Diligence)	• Validation of information technology and information technology-dependent assumptions in the investment thesis • Preliminary design of the combined information technology function (people, process, and technology) • Refinement of labor and capital estimates • Preliminary definition of transitional information technology services, including timetable and costs (if applicable)	• Refined estimates of synergies and integration costs (within and outside the information technology department) • Changes to integration assumptions developed prior to due diligence • Preliminary integration plan identifying key changes in people, process, and technology within the information technology function and technology-driven changes within other departments • Key activities to take place prior to or on day one of the integration • Preliminary service definitions, service levels, durations, and costs for an information technology transition services agreement (if applicable)

EXHIBIT 14.3   IT Involvement & Focus: Pre-Signing Phase

Transaction Phase	Information Technology Involvement	Key Information Technology Outputs
Pre-Closing (Detailed Integration Planning and Confirmatory Due Diligence)	• Development of final synergy estimates and associated information technology costs • Detailed information technology integration planning and subject-matter input into other departments' integration plans • Development of interim (transitional) and long-term information technology functions (people, process, and technology) • Drafting of information technology transition services agreements in conjunction with legal counsel	• Committed integration costs and synergies within or driven by the information technology department • Information technology integration plan • Information technology integration team and roles/responsibilities • Day one action plan

EXHIBIT 14.4   IT Involvement & Focus: Pre-Closing Phase

investment thesis to identify potential IT impacts, actions, and measurements of success, enterprises can start planning earlier and produce better results.

Exhibits 14.5 and 14.6 show a framework and example that enterprises can leverage to jump-start IT integration planning at even the earliest stages of an integration transaction.

Component of Investment Thesis	Potential Information Technology Impact	Required Integration Action(s) and Timing	Success Measures
25% Reduction in Sales, General, and Administrative Costs	DIRECT: 50% reduction in combined information technology staff with no reduction in service levels	Consolidation onto a single enterprise requirements planning (ERP) platform within six months	50% reduction in number of platforms, applications, administrative personnel, and help desk staff supporting ERP
	DIRECT: 33% reduction in combined non-ERP annual software maintenance fees and third-party information technology services	• Consolidate major-vendor software licenses (for example, Oracle) and renegotiate annual maintenance • Consolidate all wide-area network spans on a single vendor (ABC is incumbent, but XYZ also is used) and renegotiate	• 20% or greater reduction in per-user, per-seat, or per-site annual maintenance • At least a 20% reduction in annual cost per span with no more than a 24-month contract extension

EXHIBIT 14.5   IT Integration Planning Framework Example

Component of Investment Thesis	Potential Information Technology Impact	Required Integration Action(s) and Timing	Success Measures
25% Reduction in Sales, General, and Administrative Costs	INDIRECT: 33% reduction in combined accounts payable staff	• Extension of existing software-enabled auto-matching and payment authorization with incoming preferred vendors • Implementation of digital document management system to enable on-screen matching for the combined accounts payable staff	• At least 25% of incoming preferred vendors auto-matched, allowing reduction of two accounts payable staff • 30% or greater increase in number of manual invoice matches per day, allowing reduction of two additional accounts payable staff

EXHIBIT 14.6   IT Integration Planning Framework Example

Exhibit 14.5 demonstrates a process of defining and planning specific actions by the IT function to support hypothetical components of an investment thesis by introducing direct improvements within the IT function itself, as well as associated actions, timings, and success measures. Such direct IT impacts often form an important component of immediate or short-term savings to be realized following the close of the transaction. Exhibit 14.6, on the other hand, demonstrates a process by which IT executives can abstract aspects of the investment thesis that are not related to IT directly, and identify longer-term (and often more substantial) opportunities to leverage existing or potential IT investments to bring additional value through the integration process. These indirect IT impacts often are larger than the direct IT impacts and can create value not originally envisioned within the investment thesis.

DAY ONE PLANNING

A critical element of IT integration often overlooked by enterprises is that many IT activities require significant advance planning and effort to be successful. Some of the most common and most critical day one activities include the following:

- Conversion to interim or go-forward banking relationships, credit card processing, and payroll processing.
- Consolidation or integration of sales, order entry, and customer support processes.
- Redirection of legacy phone numbers and systems to the interim or go-forward phone system or phone tree.
- Changes in the delivery locations, addresses, and data streams within supply and distribution chains.
- Consolidation or integration of legacy e-mail systems.
- Consolidation of web sites or redirection to interim or go-forward web sites.
- Consolidation or integration of legacy IT help desks.
- Consolidation or integration of privacy, physical security, and information security functions.

These activities are complicated enough in their own right, but they become even more complex when the integration transaction involves the purchase and integration of assets rather than going concerns or transition services being provided by a third party (e.g., a former owner). As such, day one planning for the enterprise as a whole and for the IT function in particular must begin as early as possible, and it may be necessary to begin making changes and investing working capital prior to closing. This represents a normal financial risk associated in integration transactions and should be considered part of negotiating walk-away or termination fees on the transaction's term sheet.

The success of day one often depends on having a rapid response team of IT and business professionals available, which can require temporary resources to fill the day-to-day responsibilities of those individuals. This is often more pronounced within the IT function than elsewhere in the business because of the dual role of IT as a vertical department and an underlying foundation supporting all of the enterprise's operations.

Similarly, throughout the integration effort, the IT function will have two primary roles:

1. Completing the IT integration (people, process, and technology) as defined in the IT integration plan.
2. Supporting all of the other integration efforts being undertaken by the enterprise.

These two roles often are conflicting and may put IT leadership in the position of having to make decisions that could significantly impact the timetable, effectiveness, and results of an integration process.

For example, the IT integration plan may call for the retirement of one legacy sales order entry system and the migration of historical transactions, customer information, product and price lists, and entry of new orders to the new sales order entry system within the first 30 days of the transaction. However, as the integration progresses, the sales leaders grow concerned that there may be a temporary dip in sales as the incoming sales representatives learn the new process and system and ask to operate both systems concurrently for an additional 60 to 90 days.

In this example, a choice must be made between the incremental costs within the IT function to retain and support the legacy sales order entry system (plus the diversion of resources intended to support other integration activities) and the potential reduction in revenues resulting from the lost sales. This can put IT in a difficult position, in which the IT executive is overruled, and this endangers not only this aspect of the integration but also the results of the integration as a whole.

To minimize this type of situation and reduce the potential of an integration process going awry as the IT function is pulled in conflicting directions over multiple issues, there are two steps that enterprises should take when forming their IMOs:

1. Segregate responsibility for each of the two primary IT roles during the integration by creating a functional (vertical) IT integration leader as a

peer to the other functional (vertical) integration leaders and an IT integration enablement leader who reports directly to the IMO team leader or sponsor. When a potential issue such as the example described above arises, the IT integration enablement leader (who may not be an IT executive but should be familiar with the operations of an IT department) will assess the situation and associated risks to the integration effort and either make a binding decision or propose a solution for review and approval by the IMO team leader or sponsor.

2. Plan to add between one-half and one FTE of contract resources within each major group within the IT function to allow the leaders of those groups to be able to drop everything and engage in the support of situations such as the example described above or any other unexpected complication in the implementation of the integration plan. The ability to mobilize a rapid response team will significantly increase the potential that such events have minimal impact and are addressed both quickly and responsibly.

THE THREE RISKS

Even with all of these practices in place, there are three key risks to IT integration that enterprises should be aware of and actively seek to minimize at all stages of integration planning and execution:

1. Questions about which information systems are to survive often are raised by business integration leaders as a proxy for questions about which operational policies and practices (and therefore leadership roles) will survive. The usual assumption that all things related to the acquiring company (culture, process, leadership) will dominate in the planning and execution of the integration can lead to missed opportunities for savings, synergies, or quicker realization of value. Before making blanket decisions about information systems, it is important to revisit the investment thesis and decide which overall operations approach (including supporting information systems) will yield the best short-term and long-term results.

2. Even the most dedicated and energized IT functions have limits on their capabilities dictated by its size, composition, and budget. Assumptions by integration leaders elsewhere in the business that "IT can handle it" or "IT will figure it out" when addressing integration challenges are specious and can lead to the failure of critical elements of the overall integration plan.

The IT function should always be given the opportunity to estimate the effect on the resources and the budget required to address integration challenges, and integration leadership should be open to increasing the resources or budget available to the IT function to address them.

3. IT professionals are uniquely mobile and often can source equivalent positions outside their industry or competency with relative ease, even in a depressed economy. As many IT functions have become gradually leaner, the potential for key-person reliances within IT functions are more numerous, and the loss of a resource, even at a comparatively low level of seniority or rank, can be disastrous.

While stay bonuses and other financial incentives can help to reduce the risk that a critical resource is lost, enterprises also should be creative about motivating retention (interim and long-term) of IT staff by offering learning opportunities, operational rotations, and responsibility for new technologies) as part of their tenure.

CHAPTER CHECKLIST

After reading this chapter, keep these things on your integration check-list:

☐ Make sure IT is included as part of due diligence and pre-planning activities.
☐ Include IT as part of detailed functional day one planning.
☐ Ensure that IT is well represented in your IMO in both the IT and in other functions (e.g., HR, finance).

SUMMARY

Half or even more of the potential synergies resulting from an integration are related to or dependent on IT. No matter how contrary doing so may be to an enterprise's culture, it is important to invest sufficient resources, budget, and attention in IT before and during an integration to maximize the potential that all those synergies will be realized.

The next chapter explores how to optimize future integration through feedback tools and also explores various M&A integration lessons learned.

CHAPTER 15

Integration Feedback: Lessons Learned

In this chapter, you will learn the following:

- How to collect feedback and assess your integration efforts.
- Lessons from past integrations.

I received a good piece of advice from a manager once: Feedback is a gift. This goes for integration feedback as well.

Any process improvement person worth his or her daily rate can tell you that getting after-action feedback and data ensures that you will improve and optimize your operations. For companies with fairly frequent merger and acquisition activity, getting post-integration feedback is critical to ensuring that you are continually improving.

In effective integration planning, the feedback stage is referred to as *lessons learned*.

GOALS AND TOOLS OF LESSONS LEARNED

Collecting feedback from all stakeholder groups to continually optimize your integration strategies and tactics can include the following steps:

- At day 100, initiate a formal process to collect feedback from IMO participants and acquired company employees.
- Distribute an employee survey. It should be developed and administered through HR and implemented after any downsizing or reductions in force.

- Make sure the IMO facilitates a lessons-learned meeting with IMO participants and functional leaders to explore the following questions:
  - What integration practices, tools, and processes worked well, and why?
  - What integration practices, tools, and processes need improvement?
  - What communication vehicles worked well?
  - Did the stakeholders feel well-informed through all stages of the integration?
  - Were integration priorities clearly communicated during the integration?
  - Were success stories highlighted and people recognized?

These are just some sample questions to help you get started. You can work closely with your HR and IMO team to develop a tailored questionnaire to address all the key areas of your particular integration planning and execution.

GETTING FEEDBACK AND MAKING ADJUSTMENTS

Because integration work is extremely hectic and occurs during a very tumultuous time for a company, you need to make sure you collect feedback so you can make any midcourse corrections. Integration work is often so new for most people that they don't really know what to suggest in the first place, so sometimes you really need to push to solicit feedback.

The information you collect will be invaluable for the future integration work your organization may undertake. Collect and document all survey results and informal feedback where it can be shared and accessed by others.

Here are a few areas where integrations tend to fall short. Take these into consideration toward improvements you can make for your next integration.

Too Much Paperwork

If you are having your integration leaders for each function use regular desktop software (like Excel) for keeping their plans up-to-date, things may get a bit cumbersome—especially if there is a significant number of projects and initiatives for their functional areas.

One option to consider next time is some collaboration software that is specifically designed for integration and project management work, like Daptiv or Inchieve, which can be customized based on your integration needs and is very user-friendly. It takes a bit of getting used to if you have never used a project management tool before, but once you get acclimated, you will find it to be a time saver that helps to keep your integration work better organized.

Reconciling Integration Work with Your Day Job

Many times it is difficult to get integration leaders who can focus 100 percent on integration work. The trade-off, then, is that they keep some current responsibilities and try to juggle both jobs as best they can.

As discussed in previous chapters, the best way to solve this problem is to secure 100 percent of the person's time for integration work right off the bat, so you can completely avoid this problem. Integration work is complex and time-consuming and requires extreme focus for 90 to 120 days. If you need to compromise, negotiate for 100 percent of that person's time for at least 60 days, then revisit the situation to see if the person can take on additional responsibilities based on the progress of the work streams. For some functions, the bulk of the work may get done early, freeing the person up for his or her day job responsibilities.

Working Together

When two organizations come together, often people who don't know one another are forced to work together, and this can cause anxiety and stress. If you have an IMO with a good number of functional integration leaders who have never worked together before, create an opportunity for an ice-breaking session with some type of activity so people can get to know one another. If you have just a few new people in a group, make it your responsibility to introduce them to everyone and help them to meet everyone they will be working with.

People will be more effective once they get to know whom they are working with and feel more comfortable. In most cases, it will be IMO leaders who need to facilitate this activity. Keep your eyes and ears open for these kinds of issues so you can make midcourse adjustments and optimize your approach for your next integration.

COLLECTING POST-INTEGRATION FEEDBACK

Exhibit 15.1 shows a sample employee survey to collect post-integration feedback. It is strongly recommended that you partner with your HR leaders to develop and implement a survey using whatever methods they recommend to ensure adequate participation. There are also numerous outside survey

SAMPLE Employee Survey	Deal A	Deal B	Deal C
Question	Average	Average	Average
Communication			
There is a clear, articulated approach to the integration process			
I have received information I needed about the integration at the right time			
I have received information I needed about the integration in the most effective manner			
I am communicated with candidly at work			
Our culture supports open communication			
Communication Average			
Customer Focus			
Making the customer #1 is Company A's primary goal			
Company A considers the customer in every decision			
Customer Focus Average			
Leadership			
The appropriate people provide specific input into what and how transitions and changes are implemented			
I can expect to get the training needed to perform my job successfully after this integration			
Leadership Average			
Process & Systems Business productivity is not suffering during the integration			
Our processes will make this integration easy			
Our systems (for example, billing, order entry, provisioning) will make this integration easy			
Any problems this integration creates will be addressed			
Since the integration, I have more work than I can effectively handle			
Process & Systems Average			
Resilience			
Morale in our work unit is good			
I am willing to accept changes if it helps to improve Company A's performance			
I can cope effectively in ambiguous or uncertain job situations			
I have effective coping mechanisms to help relieve stress during this integration			
Resilience Average			
5 - Strongly Agree			
4 - Agree			
3 - Neutral			
2 - Disagree			
1 - Strongly Disagree			

EXHIBIT 15.1 Sample Employee Survey

tools available, and some corporate intranets include employee survey functionality you can use for these kinds of information-gathering exercises.

Be sure to include a good sampling of stakeholders affected by your integration activity, specifically the following:

- Senior management.
- IMO team members.
- Acquiring and acquired employees (or employees from both merged companies).
- Consultants involved in various stages of due diligence and integration planning and execution.

ADDITIONAL TIPS

Here are some additional tips, lessons learned, and other anecdotes I have gleaned from previous integrations that might be useful to you during different facets of your integration planning.

Lack of Air Cover

It is critical that the IMO report to a high-ranking executive, preferably a C-suite executive.

Integrations will inevitably bring to the surface issues no one expected, and that will require senior-level intervention. Many times someone will have to make a judgment call, since you will have competing viewpoints and an operational stalemate. These must be prioritized and expedited quickly, and having the IMO report to the C-suite makes this much easier to handle.

Undercommunicating

Sometimes leaders think that they are the only ones who need to know what's going on and that the rest of a team can be left in the dark. However, when most people are uncertain about their company's direction or their role in it, they freeze, and productivity plummets.

As we have discussed throughout this book, make sure you communicate early and often during the entire integration, and set up tools to do so.

Too Many Outside Consultants, Not Enough Insiders

I was once asked to join an integration late in the process because it was behind schedule, only to find that the IMO was being run by an entry-level consultant left behind by the large consulting firm that had helped the acquiring company with the deal transaction.

The consultant was very smart and had diplomas from some great schools, but he was inexperienced and had lost credibility among the functional team members he was working with.

The lesson here: Don't staff your IMO solely with consultants. Use them for support when necessary, but make sure you have personnel from one of the merged or acquiring companies as part of your IMO.

Be a Good Cop *and* a Bad Cop

IMO leaders have to support the new company, but they also need to quickly isolate the people who are not cooperating. Do not tolerate detractors for long, or they will poison your efforts and undermine your integration planning and execution. Get ahead of this by suggesting that the person talk to senior management or by formally recommending that the person be redeployed.

Open-Door Policy

As discussed, integrations can be tough because people are often losing their jobs or their status or are being relocated (or all three!). Therefore, I have a rule when I'm on-site at the acquired company during integration work: open doors.

Unless privacy is absolutely necessary, I make sure that the doors to any conference and war rooms we are occupying are always open, so the employees can see us working and not feel any more anxious than they already are. New faces and closed doors make people nervous. Try to avoid this whenever you can and be accessible for those who just need to talk or ask questions.

Avoid Company Politics

One of the biggest traps in integrating merging companies is getting sucked into company politics. I always remind team members that even though people will share company gossip, they are better off refocusing conversations to integration business and avoiding company politics.

This particular issue occurs often and can be extremely distracting. Listen, but don't take sides or advocate a position unless it directly affects an integration work stream or key deliverable.

Do Your Homework

Even though you may be working for an acquiring company, do some homework and get to know the acquired or merged company before you get on-site—and this means more than just the due diligence information.

Know how long the acquired company has been in business, what it produces, or what services it provides. This is so easy today, given our digital access, that not boning up on a company is inexcusable. People will appreciate the fact that you made the effort, and, most important, it will inform your integration planning efforts considerably.

Have a Bias for Urgency

Integrations should be fast paced and methodical with a bias for urgency. Has an issue come up in the morning? Get it resolved by that afternoon and then communicate the next steps. Keep moving. There is nothing worse than an integration that plods along and undermines momentum. In fact, there's an affliction called *integration fatigue* that occurs when integration work goes on too long and IMO leaders and functional team members get bored and want to do *anything* else. Integrations should have an end and it should be as soon as prudently possible.

Don't Try to Solve Everything

Sometimes integration activity becomes a home for all the ills and aspirations of an acquired organization. Because there's so much activity and muscle being expended, people think any problem can be solved during an integration process.

Don't let integration "scope creep" load your integration work plan with projects that are organizational initiatives and not integration initiatives. Here are a few examples of scope creep projects to be cautious of, including as part of integration work streams:

- Big IT system implementations.
- Strategic projects that would occur with or without integration (e.g., store redesign).
- Employee training projects that are not related to training newly acquired or merged employees.

Dispense with the Politics

Integrations can be very contentious political processes, but integration leaders need to be apolitical and rise above the day-to-day political morass. If you don't rise above it, you will lose momentum and be perceived as just another cog in the new wheel, not a catalyst for the new organization.

Be Inspirational and Lead

Integrations are tough for almost all employees on both sides of a merger or an acquisition. You can help integrations most by being a proactive, positive integration leader and an active problem solver for the new organization. People will appreciate it immensely, and it will help to keep your integration team focused and engaged.

CHAPTER CHECKLIST

Here are some key areas to focus on to help assess your integration:

- ☐ Make adjustments during your integration by collecting feedback and input at regular intervals.
- ☐ Create post-integration stakeholder surveys around day 100.
- ☐ Collect and document lessons learned so you can share and let them inform your next integration planning effort.

SUMMARY

In this chapter, we learned how to collect feedback and assess your integration efforts.

The next chapter includes an aggregated integration approach and offers various tools and templates in a standardized playbook you can use to help your organization manage integration activity in an organized and methodical fashion.

CHAPTER 16

Creating an Integration Playbook

The following is a sample playbook, an aggregation of many of the tools and much of the advice offered in this book. The purpose of this playbook is to give you an idea of how all of the integration plan elements can be packaged together to help you involve the stakeholders who will become a successful part of your integration project.

If your organization is going to be integrating merged or acquired companies frequently, having a working playbook is a good idea. However, playbooks are fluid and never complete; they should continually be optimized by lessons learned from previous integrations.

I'm amazed when I talk to companies that have frequent integration activities but have no standardized approach. It's an exercise in reinventing the wheel each time there's an integration activity. Integration work is hard enough as it is, so developing a playbook will help your company adopt some standardized and repeatable processes and tools it can leverage for future integration activities.

Keep in mind that it is important to create something that can aggregate organizational competency, like a playbook, but that it should be continually improved and updated after each integration.

PLAYBOOK CONTENTS

A typical playbook's contents might look like the following lists that show some of the most common topics discussed in this book. These are presented in a fairly intuitive order, based on the key planning phases.

Setup, Planning, and Execution

Purpose and scope. These parts of the playbook help you to establish what the official role of your playbook will be to support your organization's integration activity and how the playbook elements all fit together. Consider these sections a "playbook 101" overview:

Playbook scope

Relationship between playbook elements

Integration management plan. These sections detail how to set up an IMO and some suggestions on integration governance:

Organization

Governance

Integration planning processes. These sections detail the primary integration phases (e.g., pre-planning, execution) and repositories for due diligence checklists and formats for initial integration plans:

Integration phases overview

Collecting planning inputs (due diligence checklist)

Initial integration plan

Execution and monitoring processes. These parts of the playbook consist of the following:

Integration program management

Program management processes

Specific Phases and Key Special Needs

These sections delve deeper into the important areas discussed in this book. If your organization has unique integration needs based on industry and acquisition strategy specifics, this is the area of your playbook where you would include any additional playbook elements.

Integration project closing

End state tracking process

Lessons learned process

Communication management plan (CMP)

CMP objectives and guiding principles

CMP processes

CMP matrix: messages and stakeholders

Synergy management plan (SMP)

Synergy initiative planning

Synergy initiative process management

Culture and talent assessment plan (CTAP)

Culture assessment

Talent assessment

Retention and separation

Playbook training

Often overlooked is the fact that an integration playbook is a new tool and that anyone using it requires some training. The playbook is intended to be not an instruction manual but more of a reference guide to speed understanding as well as tool and template development.

Make sure that anyone assigned to the IMO who is going to leverage an integration playbook has the benefit of some training and has time to digest and fully understand all of the playbook elements and how they work together.

PLAYBOOK ELEMENTS

The ideal playbook for your organization should be informed by key planning dimensions, including the following considerations by subject (as part of the contents just outlined):

Playbook Purpose

- Creating a compilation of integration best practices that can be utilized by company executives. This can save them time so management can focus on driving business results.
- Providing flexible and scalable integration tools, templates, and processes that foster integration consistency across all company divisions.
- Creating a shared service to help company management with integration activity.

Playbook Synergy Program Management Goals

- Creating clear outlines of synergy and business benefit realizations.
- Identifying and incorporating short-term synergies into an integration plan.
- Identifying and transferring long-term synergy targets to new functional owners.

Operating Results and Productivity

- Remembering that no disruption to the acquired business means that productivity remains constant or improves.
- Outlining operational measurements of the acquired business.

Organizational Effectiveness and Employee Satisfaction

- Creating outlines of established authority chains. Make sure there are no reporting gaps or duplications.
- Confirming that employees are accepting of change by enacting satisfaction surveys.
- Continually customizing and optimizing your playbook based on your company's:
  - Merger type
  - Industries
  - Frequency of activity
  - Organizational design
  - Specific business goals and objectives

Scope

- Making sure the integration playbook you are utilizing is approved by company management.
- Making sure your integration support time frame begins 30 days before closing and averages 90 to 120 days after closing in duration.
- Making sure your integration playbook supports multiple integration scenarios.
- Remembering that some integrations may require ad hoc support or augmentation to account for unique integration scenarios and planning needs.

Exhibit 16.1 shows how the scoping process fits within a typical integration time frame.

	Due Diligence	Integration		End State Monitoring
Goal	Value Preservation		Value Creation	
When	Pre-Close	First 30 Days	30 – 100 Days	> 100 Days
Activities	• Finalize integration project scope • If possible, scope any ad hoc integration planning requirements			

EXHIBIT 16.1 IMO Duration

HOW THE ELEMENTS WORK TOGETHER

Exhibit 16.2 is shows how all of the playbook elements work together and form a continuous feedback loop for ongoing playbook optimization.

Your playbook should be informed by seven primary sources of information.

1. *Acquisition strategy.* As discussed earlier in this book, there are several different types of acquisition models, but if your company has a particular model, you can create a playbook customized for that particular approach.
2. *Due diligence information.* Chapter 6 includes comprehensive lists of typical due diligence information, and the output of the due diligence process should be used to inform your playbook. There may be particular areas of due diligence output that are standard for a particular industry, and you can make that a more standardized, template-driven deliverable.
3. *Integration scope.* Essentially, this is what the role of the IMO and the playbook is as part of your company's integration strategy.
4. *Pre-closing planning processes.* This is the collective activity that occurs prior to day 0, or closing day, which is when the official change of control takes place. The pre-planning activity outlined in Chapter 5 is what should be completed prior to day 0.

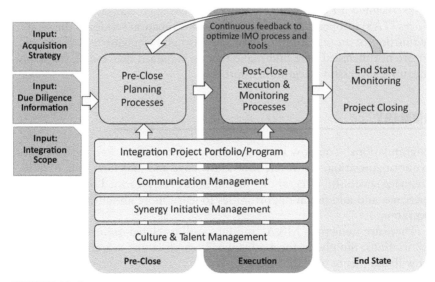

EXHIBIT 16.2 Playbook Elements and Continuous Optimization

5. *Post-closing execution and monitoring processes.* These are all of the IMO execution processes, including communication planning, synergy plan management, and culture and talent assessment activities.
6. *End state monitoring.* This is the transition point, when the bulk of integration activity is completed and the remaining projects or initiatives transition into the end state process.
7. *Project closing.* Integration work is completed and the IMO officially disbands.

APPLYING THE PLAYBOOK

This playbook should be used to help structure a consistent integration approach and be used to guide execution. However, every company's integration activity will be somewhat unique, so you need to be flexible as there may be parts of this playbook that need various degrees of emphasis.

There may also be parts of the playbook you just don't need (e.g., an extensive talent assessment) because it's out of scope or being handled by another department.

As mentioned, an integration playbook such as this should be continually updated and improved with lessons learned from your integration activity. Technically, an integration playbook is never done; it should be considered a living document.

When you use an integration playbook, there should also be someone clearly in charge of the playbook and its continued development. Typical groups assigned for this type of activity may be called transaction advisory services (TAS) or operations, or sometimes this function resides in the strategy function of an organization. You can also add elements to a playbook that are not included here and make them a standard deliverable for your company's successful integration approach.

SUMMARY

Congratulations! You now know more about integration than most people in your organization. However, your knowledge and understanding of how to manage successful integrations should always be informed by real-world experience and additional opportunities to learn more about the subject of integration.

There are numerous M&A- and integration-related online forums and organizations. Simply perform a keyword search in any search engine and you will find plenty of viable options.

Good luck with your integration!

About the Author

Scott Whitaker is the president and CEO of Whitaker & Company, an Atlanta-based consulting and project management firm specializing in helping companies to develop, execute, and implement merger integrations and business strategies designed to achieve growth.

Since 2005, Whitaker & Company has been involved in merger integration and strategy and operations projects totaling more than $25 billion for both domestic and international companies.

Whitaker & Company helps companies to realize the goals of their M&A strategies by creating customized, flexible, and scalable integration playbooks as well as detailed operational and functional integration plans with tools, templates, and reports to support flawless execution. For more company information, please visit http://www.whitakercompany.com. You can also visit http://www.integrationplaybook.com for additional material related to this book.

Prior to starting Whitaker & Company, Scott held senior-level marketing, sales, and operations positions with several Fortune 500 companies, and his experience includes:

- Developing branding strategies and marketing plans for companies in the hospitality, financial service, consumer durables, and communications industries.
- Managing launch and start-up operations, including retail site selection, capex funding requirements, staff recruitment, and market level strategy.
- Leading consumer and business-to-business sales teams over diverse geographic territories and competitive landscapes.
- Developing customer acquisition and marketing promotion programs for retail store chains and major national retailers.
- Creating and leading marketing departments at both the field and corporate levels.

Scott holds the certified management consultant (CMC) credential. The CMC designation is awarded only to a select group of consultants (only

10,000 worldwide) who have demonstrated that they produce substantive results, adhere to the Institute of Management Consultants (IMC) canon of ethics, and manage their practices professionally.

Scott lives in Atlanta, Georgia, with his wife, Eve, and their three children, Wyatt, Holland, and Madeline.

About the Website

Please visit http://www.wiley.com/go/integrationplaybook for access to a sample integration playbook as outlined in this book.

Feel free to refer to the online sample alongside the information in this book as you read. This will give you a better understanding of what your eventual integration playbook might look like as well as how to make sure to innovate and evolve your playbooks with each new integration.

You may also visit http://www.integrationplaybook.com to access additional tools, templates, and integration-related content.

Index

Page numbers in *italics* refer to exhibits.

Accounting and finance
  complexity of, 21–23
  executing integration plan and,
    84–85
  financial information documents,
    50
Acquisitions, defined, 7–8
Agreement (employment)
  documentation, 53
Audience, communication with.
  See Communication planning

Benefit plan documentation,
  53–54
Book, organization of, 2–4
Business case, 19–30
  challenges of integration and, *24,*
    24–29, *26, 27, 28, 29*
  complex activities and, 21–23
  for integration support, 23–24
  integration success and, 29–30
  to improve performance, 19–21
Business growth, talent assessment
  criteria and, *118, 119*
Business management, talent
  assessment criteria, *120*
Business plans
  due diligence and, 51
  executing integration plan and,
    81
Bylaws, 49

Change management, culture and,
  112–114
Charters
  due diligence phase, 49
  setting up an integration project
    charter, 69–72
Chief operating officers (COO),
  63–66, *65*
Clean-room planning, 40–42, 47
Closing dates, pre-planning for, 40
Collaboration software, 150–151
Communication planning, 95–106
  complexity of, 22
  executing integration plan and,
    75–76 (*See also* Execution)
  feedback for, 153
  generally, 95
  information transfer and cultural
    integration, *110*
  matrix, *97,* 97–101, *99, 100*
  objectives, 95–96
  pre-planning phase and, 41–42
  principles, 96–97
  process, 101–105, *102, 103, 104,*
    105
  See also Marketing
Company politics, avoiding, 154,
  155–156
Complexity, assessing, 11–17, *12,*
  21–23. *See also* Integration
  assessment; Risk assessment

167

Printed and bound by CPI Group (UK) Ltd, Croydon, CR0 4YY

23/04/2025

14660921-0001